BETWEEN CULTURES

ESSAYS ON LITERATURE, LANGUAGE AND EDUCATION

Distributed by :

INDIAN BOOKS CENTRE
Exporters of Indian Books
40/5, Shakti Nagar
Delhi-110007
(INDIA)

Between Cultures
Essays on Literature, Language and Education

D.C.R.A. GOONETILLEKE

Professor & Head, Dept. of English
University of Kelaniya

SRI SATGURU PUBLICATIONS
DELHI—INDIA

Published by :

© SRI SATGURU PUBLICATIONS
Indological and Oriental Publishers
40/5, Shakti Nagar
Delhi-110007
(INDIA)

First Edition : Delhi 1987

I.S.B.N. : 81-7030-089-4

Printed in India at :
A.R. Printers, D-102, New Seelampur, Delhi-110053.

To

My Parents

Contents

Acknowledgements

Acknowledgements are due to the editors of the following journals in which the essays collected in this book first appeared or have been accepted for publication :

The Journal of South Asian Literature for 'Leonard Woolf's Classic about Sri Lanka'.

Kalyani : Journal of Humanities & Social Sciences of the University of Kelaniya, Vol. 2, 1983, for 'Lester James Peries' *Village in the Jungle*'.

Navasilu V, 1983, for 'Language Planning in Sri Lanka'.

The Toronto South Asian Review and *The Journal of Commonwealth Literature* for 'Beyond Alienation : The Efflorescence of Sri Lankan Literature in English'.

Navasilu IV, 1981, for 'English for University Admission'.

The Journal of Commonwealth Literature, Vol. 7, No. 1, 1972, for 'Forgotten Nineteenth-century Fiction : William Arnold's *Oakfield* and William Knighton's *Forest Life in Ceylon*'.

A Review of International English Literature, Vol. 5, No. 4, 1974, for 'Colonial Neuroses : Kipling and Forster'.

The Kipling Journal, Vol. XLII, No. 193, 1975, for 'Kipling's Indian Poetry'.

The Sri Lanka Journal of Humanities, Vol. 2, No. 1, 1976, for 'Race Relations in Shakespeare'.

Vidyodaya Journal of Arts, Science and Letters, Vol. 6, No. 2, 1978, for 'Much Ado About Nothing Reconsidered'.

Navasilu I, 1976, for '*The Tempest*—its significance for developing countries'.

The Sri Lanka Journal of the Humanities, Vol. 5, Nos. 1 and 2, 1979, for 'Conrad as a Modernist Writer : *The Secret Agent*'.

The Sri Lanka Journal of the Humanities Vol. 1, No. 1, 1975, for 'Conrad's *Victory* Reconsidered'.

Kalyani : Journal of Humanities and Social Sciences of the University of Kelaniya, Vol. 1, Nos. 1 and 2, 1982, for 'George Orwell's *Burmese Days* : The Novelist as Reformer' ; the present expanded version appeared in the E.F.C. Ludowyk felicitation volume.

Preface

This book presents a selection made from essays published between 1971 and 1984 or accepted for publication. They were all written after I had read for my Ph.D., after I felt I had something of my own to contribute to English studies and education. I have been impressed by F.R. Leavis' advocacy of Cambridge 'English' as the mainstay and focus of humane education. The 'New Criticism', as generally practised, had the virtue of emphasizing the intrinsic aesthetic qualities of literary works, but it was inclined to treat these works as if they were composed outside the circumstances of history and the lives of writers. Clearly, art reflects the age and the life of the artist, which shaped it. I have tried to digest the major virtue of the 'New Criticism' and avoid its grave failing. I approach literature as art in the context of relevant historical and biographical facts.

Such an approach, if it is to be profitable, has to be, in the first place, inspired and controlled by a literary critical sense. Then, we must be aware of the complexities of the relation between the world of the imagination and the world of historical and biographical facts. For one thing, far from all the facts are relevant ; we need a sense of what facts had most to do with fashioning the work of art. For another thing, facts, as they strike the imagination and are organized by it, undergo decisive selection and shaping. Thus, to treat, say, Kipling, Forster and Cary as "chroniclers of British expansion" is to overlook these complexities, to equate erroneously the world of the imagination with the world of facts, to confuse the ways of the artist with the methods of the historian.

Many of my essays are on English literature, as it strikes a critic from the Asian region, aware of cultures in the West and East. I have been studying Sri Lankan literature too because I feel it is not only the duty and obligation of a critic to come to terms with the literature of his own country but necessary if he is to keep his feet on the ground and achieve fulfilment. The essays on Language Planning and English at the level of university admission arose out of a sense that our English programmes were heading towards a national disaster and that the crisis should be averted. The essays on Sri Lankan topics are relevant to other developing countries because the Third World has much in common. But I am not offering all these essays as a Sri Lankan or Asian or Third World critic but as a member of an international community of scholars ; that, ultimately, is how we should see our task.

D.C.R.A. Goonetilleke

University of Kelaniya,
Sri Lanka.
1986.

CHAPTER 1

Leonard Woolf's classic about Sri Lanka

Leonard Woolf and E.M. Forster were close friends. Forster has said that he probably would not have completed *A Passage to India* without the encouragement of Woolf.[1] Forster's novel set in India soon achieved fame and was widely read. But Woolf's novel set in Sri Lanka, *The Village in the Jungle*, is still comparatively unknown outside the island, though reprinted several times in Britain[2] and though it does not deserve obscurity and neglect. It is most outstanding creative work in English about Sri Lanka and the touchstone of artistic distinction for Sri Lankan literature in English. I also think that it transcends its local significance. I propose to introduce it to new readers and make a case for it as a genuinely tragic novel which has both local and universal relevance ; in a word, a minor classic.

1

In one way, Leonard Woolf is squarely in the tradition of British fiction about developing countries, a valuable tradition which includes Joseph Conrad, Rudyard Kipling, E.M. Forster, Joyce Cary and Graham Greene. Their experiences abroad were crucial to their development. Joseph Conrad told Edward Garnett : "Before the Congo I was only a simple animal".[3] Forster considers his stay in Dewas State Senior "the great opportunity of my life".[4] Similarly, Leonard Woolf confesses in *Growing* :

> I had entered Ceylon as an imperialist, one of the white rulers of our Asiatic Empire. The curious thing is that I was not aware of this. The horrible urgency of politics after the 1914 war, which forced every intelligent person to be passionately interested in them, was unknown to my generation at Cambridge. Except for the Dreyfus case and

> one or two other questions, we were not deeply concerned with politics. That is why I could take a post in the Ceylon Civil Service without any thought about its political aspect. Travelling to Jaffna in January 1905, I was a very innocent, unconscious imperialist. What is perhaps interesting in my experience during the next six years is that I saw from the inside British imperialism at its apogee and that I gradually became fully aware of its nature and problems.[5]

Thus Woolf responds to Ceylon as a Wasterner, as an alien, and his experience here makes him maturer.

Though an alien, Woolf's insight into, and concern for, indigenous life are such that he can write a novel wholly about indigenous living with only indigenous people as his major characters. He is closer to the Ceylonese than Forster is to the Indians. In *A Passage to India*, the two most important characters are British: in social matters its central character is Fielding, in metaphysical matters Mrs. Moore. The important Indian characters such as Aziz, Hamidullah, even Professor Godbole are educated, Westernized and belong to the middle class. In the novel, the common people are no more important as individuals than the punkah-puller. Woolf, in fact, is more akin to Joyce Cary than to Forster. The chief characters of three out of Cary's four African novels are Nigerians, Aissa in *Aissa Saved,* Louis Aladai in *The African Witch* and Mister Johnson. But these three Nigerians are more or less educated and more or less Westernized ; indeed, Louis Aladai had been educated at Oxford University. It is true that Cary shows a fine open-minded interest in African culture, a culture very different from the British at an earlier stage of development, rather like the openness we feel in Forster's account of the Hindu festivities in the last part of *A Passage to India.* Yet I do not know of any British writer who has come consistently closer than Woolf to the common people of a developing country. All his major characters—not only the 'hero' Silindu and the 'Villain' Babehami—are uneducated peasants. Babehami is the only villager with a claim to 'education' and he can do no more educationally than write his name. It is the indigenous quality of *The Village in the Jungle* that makes it an integral part of the tradition of Sri Lankan fiction in English, while it remains at the same time an integral part of a British tradition.

2

The action of *The Village in the Jungle* moves outside Beddagama, but Beddagama is its main setting. It is a remote, rather isolated village in the Hambantota district and, when Woolf focuses attention on it, it is as though he is directing a spotlight on an area. Yet remoteness and isolation are far from all. The conditions in and around the village are dreadful. The village is surrounded by jungle and the jungle continually threatens to overrun it. Woolf says: "All jungles are evil, but no jungle is more evil than that which lay about the village of Beddagama".[6] The "evil" does not remain an empty abstract exaggeration. It is suggested by an exemplum strategically placed at the beginning of the action—the story of the hunter and tracker of game who "had boasted that their was no fear in the jungle and in the end the jungle took him" (p. 3). The "evil" of the jungle is made concrete by Woolf's description :

> The trees are stunted and twisted by the drought, by the thin and sandy soil, by the dry wind. They are scabrous, thorny trees, with grey leaves whitened by the clouds of dust which the wind perpetually sweeps over them : their trunks are grey with hanging, stringy lichen. And there are enormous cactuses, evil-looking and obscene, with their great fleshy green slabs, which put out immense needle-like spines. More evil-looking still are the great leafless trees, which look like a tangle of gigantic spiders' legs—smooth, bright green, jointed together—from which, when they are broken, oozes out a milky, viscous fluid. (p. 4).

Woolf's style appears simple because its effects do not seem injected and obtrusive. But it is cunningly wrought and has a subtle rhetorical power. The description is accurate and has touches of illuminating imagery. Woolf seems to respond to the jungle as if it were a living monster and the jungle is indeed a palpable presence of this kind throughout the novel. He goes on to define key traits of the jungle :

> For the rule of jungle is first fear, and then hunger and thirst. (p. 5).

The fear, hunger and thirst are precisely and amply illustrated : the deer, driven by their thirst, come down timorously to the water-hole ; there is fear in the leopard's eyes and in his slinking feet ; and so on.

The jungle becomes, in P.K. Elkin's phrase, "a symbol of the cruelty of nature".[7] But its full significance entails a paradox. As the sea is to the fishing community in Synge's *Riders to the Sea*, the jungle is the greatest source of danger to the villagers and, at the same time, their key source of livelihood. They lived mainly by a kind of primitive agriculture : 'they cultivated rice about once in ten years and usually the village lived entirely by cultivating chenas' (p. 10). They supplemented their meagre agricultural produce by hunting, by plucking jungle fruits and getting edible leaves from the jungle. Their medicine was herbs from the jungle. Thus, the evil of the jungle has an ironical dimension.

The cultural gulf between Woolf and the villagers of Beddagama involves considerable difficulties of understanding and presentation. At the same time, Woolf's choice of these villagers as his major characters has advantages. Woolf gains the same advantage Wordsworth does, when the latter dissatisfied with the sophistication of townsmen, turns to "low and rustic life" : "in that situation our elementary feelings exist is a state of greater simplicity and consequently may be more accurately contemplated and more forcibly communicated".[8] In addition, Woolf's villagers are at an earlier stage of development than Wordsworth's rustics and are hardly civilized. Thus, in Beddagama our feelings exist in a much greater state of simplicity. The attraction of Africa for Joyce Cary is like the attraction of Beddagama for Woolf : 'basic obsessions are there seen naked in bold and dramatic action'.[9]

Elementary human feelings appear naked in Woolf's villagers and are also severely tested because their conditions of life are terribly difficult. Woolf sees a similarity between life in the jungle and life in the village :

> And just as in the jungle fear and hunger for ever crouch, slink, and peer with every beast, so hunger and the fear of hunger always lay upon the village. (p. 11).

Indeed, the jungle is the central shaping influence of the village :

> The spirit of the jungle is in the village, and in the people who live in it. They are simple, sullen, silent men. In their faces you can see plainly the fear and hardship of their lives. They are very near to the animals which live in the jungle around them. They look at you with the melancholy and patient stupidity of the buffalo in their eyes, or the cunning of the jackal. And there is in them the blind anger of the jungle, the ferocity of the leopard, and the sudden fury of the bear. (pp. 11-2).

Woolf tends to speak of animals as if they were human beings and the rustics as if they were animals. This is not a mere literary device which lends vividness to his characterization of animals and people. This suggests the basic oneness between animals and human beings at a primitive stage.

The animal imagery in the novel is important and pervasive. It gives *The Village in the Jungle* a symbolic dimension. As in Emily Bronte's *Wuthering Heights*, the symbolism in *The Village in the Jungle* is interwoven with actuality.

> Nanchohami had touched the mainspring upon which the life of the village worked—debt. The villagers lived upon debt, and their debts were the main topic of their conversation. A good kurakkan crop, from two to four acres of chena, would be sufficient to support a family for a year. But no one, not even the headman, ever enjoyed the full crop which he had reaped. At the time of reaping a band of strangers from the little town of Kamburupitiya, thirty miles away, would come into the village. Mohamadu Lebbe Ahamadu Cassim, the Moorman boutique-keeper, had supplied clothes to be paid for in grain, with a hundred per cent interest, at the time of reaping ; the fat Sinhalese Mudalali, Kodikarage Allis Appu, had supplied grain and curry stuffs on the same terms ; . . . (pp. 30-1).

Here is present a touch of inartistic explicitness in noting the role of debt in the life of the village. But the points are usually dramatized ; they reveal's Woolf's understanding of social processes. His understanding of psychological processes is equally sound. Most striking is his sense of primitive psychology, especially during the Punchirala episode. Punchirala, the ugly unscrupulous medicine–man, wants Hinnihami to be his wife. Both the woman and her father, Silindu, dislike the match. They reject Punchirala's proposal ; at the same time, they are frightened of his magical powers. Indeed, Silindu works himself into an unbalanced state ; he comes to believe that a devil has entered his body and feels that his life is slipping away. It takes a pilgrimage and the eventual surrender of Hinnihami to Punchirala to 'cure' Silindu.

3

Beddagama is primitive in that it is a small, rural, illiterate, very homogeneous community living in huts, but by the time of the action it has ceased to be wholly primitive in that it is in contact with the outer world, with 'civilization'. The influence of 'civilization' has been uneven and it is this unevenness that seems to me the source of the whole tragedy. Silindu and his family have remained jungle people, whereas their enemy Babehami has been influenced by 'civilization' and is in touch with it. As the sole representative of the Government in Beddagama, Babehami makes life difficult for Silindu and at first the jungle man is a helpless uncomprehending victim of the Headman's wiles. Babehami and Fernando, the trader from Kamburupitiya, a 'civilized' outsider, even try to frame Silindu and Babun. They succeed with Babun, but fail with Silindu. Bubun is sentenced to imprisonment for six months, while Silindu is acquitted. Silindu realizes the evil of Babehami and Fernando, and kills them both. His 'revenge' is a kind of tribal justice, but the agents of 'civilization' have to send him to prison. The village itself regresses from a semi-primitive to a primitive condition. The jungle covers the track which connected it to the outside world. Babun dies in prison. Death, disease and hunger visit the village year after year, and the few survivors migrate to Maha

Potana. Only Punchirala and Punchi Menika are left in the village to continue the hopeless struggle. Punchirala does not live long and, finally, the jungle takes Punchi Menika and obliterates the entire village. The obliteration is brought about by the interaction of a complex of forces—the outside forces of 'civilization', the frailties of primitive life and inhospitable nature.

4

The action of *The Village in the Jungle* takes place at a time when Sri Lanka was firmly under British rule. Imperialism enters the novel, but it is a secondary concern. Woolf's awareness of its evils and limitations is a finely integrated part of the novel. Imperialism spreads its tentacles into areas as remote as Beddagama. Babehami's position as Headman is part of the British administration and his tyrannical power derives from his place in the imperial system :

> The life of the village and of every man in it depended upon the cultivation of chenas . . . . The villagers owned no jungle themselves ; it belonged to the crown, and no one might fell a tree or clear a chena in it without a permit from the Government. It was through these permits that the headman had his hold upon the villagers. (pp. 33-4)

Still, Woolf's exposure of imperialism relates mainly to its system of justice. The case of Babehami and Farnando against Silindu and Babun is heard by a British judge at Kamburupitiya. He rightly acquits Silindu but wrongly convicts Babun. The judge thinks that 'there is almost certainly something behind this case which has not come out', but he does not act on this hunch. He does not understand the helplessness of the simple jungle man, Babun, against the plotting of Babehami and Fernando. There is a contrast between the sophistication of the system of justice and the simple primitiveness of the accused, a contrast which is underlined by the contrast inherent in Woolf's description of the setting for the hearing, a court-house looking out towards the jungle. The judge is right and fair according to British justice, but the system does not quite suit the needs of the 'underdeveloped' context.

5

In *The Village in the Jungle*, the 'hero' is Silindu. He leads a life cut off from the rest of the villagers of Beddagama. He was a cultivator like the others but he was the laziest among them. They called him 'tikak pissu' (slightly mad). "He seemed only at first sight a little more taciturn and inert than the other villagers. But the village had its reasons. Silindu slept with his eyes open like some animals, and very often he would moan, whine, and twitch in his sleep like a dog ; he slept as lightly as a deer, and would start up from the heaviest sleep in an instant fully awake" (p. 13). The comparisons to animals are a characteristic aspect of Woolf's portrayal of Silindu ; they underline the primitive and animal-like nature of the man. His complex of fear of and love for the jungle reflects Woolf's own response as expressed in *Growing*,[10] and this is a clue to Woolf's understanding of his hero.

In certain ways, Silindu is cast in the traditional mould of the tragic hero, whether one thinks of Greek tragedy or Shakespearean tragedy : he is a man exceptional in his society and, at the same time, he is part of common humanity. But Woolf's here is modern in a significant way : he is not a member of royalty or the upper classes, like Oedipus, Macbeth or Lear ; he is a primitive jungle man who belongs to the lower rungs even in his society. Woolf's portrayal of Silindu is supremely realistic : when his wife gives birth to twins, two girls, Silindu assaults her, crying

> 'Vesi ! vesi mau ! Where is the son who is to carry my gun into the jungle, and who will clear the chena for me ? Do you bear me vesi for me to feed and clothe and provide dowries ? Curse you !' And this was the beginning of Silindu's quarrel with Babehami, the headman ; for Babehami, hearing the cries of Dingihami, and the other women, rushed up from the adjoining compound and dragged Silindu from the house. (p. 15)

It is important to notice that in "the beginning of Silindu's quarrel with Babehami" it is Babehami who is right, not Silindu. Silindu has more faults which incur the hostility of Babehami : he is a bad and chronic debtor ; he "was too lazy even to cultivate a chena properly and even in a good year his crop was always the smallest in the village" (p. 34). Thus the contrast between Silindu and Babehami is not between a pure white hero and a completely black villain. Both have their demerits, though these are not of the same kind. Silindu's demerits can be considered shortcomings, whereas Babehami's demerits such as his cunning and unscrupulousness have the quality of evil. This accounts for the fact that we tend to sympathize with Silindu rather than Babehami.

Silindu has a fairly simple nature, characteristic of a primitive man. His 'philosophy of life' is fatalism, a view common to the villagers of Beddagama and, indeed, common to peasant life in general. It is the response of 'undeveloped' minds to the very difficult circumstances in which they are placed and which they cannot understand. When Punchi Menika wants to marry Babun and Karlinahami sides with them, Silindu's view is that "it was only one more of the evils which inevitably came upon him" (p. 62). When Punchirala wants to marry Hinnihami, he says : 'Evils come upon a man : it is fate. What can I do ?' (p. 82). Silindu's fatalism remains unchanged throughout his life, but his character does change in certain ways. He did not welcome the birth of Punchi Menika and Hinnihami, and was totally indifferent to them. But after about three years he began to love them very much. When Punchi Menika marries Babun, he transfers all his affection to Hinnihami. Hinnihami's death is a big below to him but he still has Punchi Menika. When Babehami and Fernando try to frame Silindu and Babun, Silindu's character undergoes its most significant development. He arrives at an understanding of his predicament, decides to act on his understanding and even uses guile to kill Babehami. He is relieved after he kills Babehami and Fernando, and gives himself up to the law. On his way to the Supreme Court session at Tangalle, he meets an old beggar who preaches Buddhism. He comes under the influence of the beggar's teaching ; he virtually renounces life and achieves a kind of peace even as he languishes in jail. Thus,

Silindu's character is fairly simple as well as a developing one. It measures up to the demands of a tragic hero's role in a way similar to that of a major character in Hardy's novels.

Punchi Menika and Hinnihami play prominent roles in the tragedy, though they are not quite as important as Silindu. All three form a family group which is cut off from the other villagers and they are nicknamed the 'veddas'. They are attached to each other as animals are ; Punchi Menika and Hinnihami learnt to love Silindu "blindly, as a dog loves his master" (p. 24). They have "the wildness and strangeness" (p. 52) which are part of Silindu's character. Though female, they are given a masculine training by Silindu ; they become jungle women in the same way Silindu is a jungle man. Thus Punchi Menika and Hinnihami have important qualities in common. At the same time, they are differentiated and each has a personality of her own. Punchi Menika was "a wonderful gentleness" (p. 52), whereas Hinnihami has "a violence of feeling" (p. 66) and is formidable. After she marries Babun, Punchi Menika's character changes significantly and she becomes like the other women of the village. "The simplicity of Babun reacted upon her : she became the man's woman, the cook of his food, the cleaner of his house, the bearer of his children" (p. 65). She and Babun are closely attached to each other : when Fernando wants Punchi Menika to be his mistress, neither his bribes nor his threats can break the loyalty of Punchi Menika and Babun to each other. Unfortunately, she loses Babun and Silindu and also Hinnihami, and finds it very difficult to live in Beddagama. But she is to attached to her village and too conservative to migrate. She is the last survivor of the village and the jungle takes her. Her end is pathetic, but she had known happiness, though for a short period.

Unlike Punchi Menika's, Hinnihami's character changes little. She is happy with Silindu but, when she reaches marriageable age, she is unfortunate. It is a man like Punchirala who is attracted to her. Silindu supports her when she spurns him, but Punchirala is too cunning and powerful for them. Hinnihami and Silindu finally surrender Punchirala. But Hinnihami is not afraid of Punchirala and, in fact, it is the medicine-man who comes to fear her. He does not oppose her, indeed he is relieved, when she leaves him to rejoin Silindu. Hinnihami regains happiness but only very briefly. She gives birth to a child by Punchirala but disease soon takes Punchi Nona. Hinnihami consoles herself with the deer, Punchi Appu, who had been brought to her by Silindu and whom she suckled. In fact, she had begun to care for the animal more than for her child. Yet when the villagers saw the attachment of Hinnihami and the deer, they condemn both as evil. They cruelly maim and kill the deer despite Hinnihami's attempt to save it. As a consequence, she loses the will to live. Unlike Punchi Menika, she remains a rather wild woman to the end, but her nature is no less attractive than Punchi Menika's. Her life is more unlucky than Punchi Menika's and her end is equally sad. Thus the characters of Punchi Menika and Hinnihami develop differently and their fates are different ; yet both their roles are interesting and both characters come alive.

Woolf's portrayal of Silindu, Babehami, Punchi Menika and Hinnihami reveals his understanding of various kinds of primitive Asian peasants, and demonstrates his powers of character-creation and command of character-interaction in an area of life rather unusual in first-rate literature in English. Woolf's characterization of the Sinhalese villagers has to include a rendering of their speech. The problem of language facing him differs from Forster's in *A Passage to India.* Woolf is aware that it would be false to make the Sinhalese village speak English as if he were British just as Forster knows that it would be unrealistic to put British English into the mouths of his Indian characters. But the latter has to render *the Indian kind of English* spoken by *Westernized Indians* and does so, whereas Woolf has to perform the more difficult task of fashioning an English equivalent for the Sinhalese spoken by almost all his characters. Woolf's success is evident in this brief extract from a conversation among some of the village women at the tank in Beddagama :

'Nanchohami, your tongue is still as sharp as chillies.

Punchi Menika has gone with my brother, and Hinnihami is busy in the house.'

'Punchi Menika wants but three things to make her a man. I pity you, Karlinahami, to live in the house of a madman, and to bring up his children shameless, having no children of your own. They are vedda children, and will be vedda women, wandering in the jungle like men.' (p. 27)

The speech is rooted in the jungle context through local references. The artlessness of the speech and occasional non-English turn of phrase are appropriate to the conversation of primitive women ; the non-English turns of phrase echo Sinhalese idiom. It is more difficult to present argument : here Babun wants Silindu's consent to marry Punchi Menika :

'They call us veddas in the village, while you are of the headman's house. Does the leopard of the jungle mate with the dog of the village ?' (Silindu)

'That is nothing to me. The wild buffalo seeks the cows in the village herds. The girl is very gentle, and my mind is made up. Also the girl wishes to come to me.' (Babun) (p. 59)

Woolf captures the kind of logic which is characteristic of the primitive minds of the villagers. He shows how they live so close to nature, to their jungle environment, that their thinking processes are influenced by animal life.

6

If one is asked what is *The Village in the Jungle* about, one could reply that it is, the first place, about semi-primitive life in Beddagama. Its obvious relevance would be to an understanding of other villages like Beddagama which existed and are existing in Sri Lanka and other 'undeveloped' parts of the world ; Beddagama is typical of dry-zone jungle villages. But even at the time the novel was written, Beddagama was not typical of Sri Lanka and is not presented as such. Woolf suggests in the novel that life in a city like Colombo or a small town like Kamburupitiya is very different and much easier than life in Beddagama. He also suggests that there are villages not far from Beddagama whose life is different and easier—Kotegoda, the Malay village where Punchirala's father exhibited his dark powers, and Maha Potana. Thus Beddagama is not typical of rural Sri Lanka or even of the Hambantota District. It should also be noted that villages like Beddagama were and are disappearing with the spread of civilization. Viewed in this way, the significance of the novel is very limited and dated. But its significance is universal when viewed in a deep and symbolic way. By concentrating on semi-primitive life, Woolf has been able to capture human feelings and situations which are essential and permanent. Life at Beddagama is generally a terrible struggle for existence and this view of life relates not only to life in such places. It applies to life in Sri Lanka in general, to modern life and to life in general. I am inclined to think that Woolf arrived at this view of life as a response not only to jungle life and life in Sri Lanka but to life in Europe and elsewhere, to the whole of human existence. It has been argued by Yasmine Gooneratne that Woolf's novel unconsciously influenced T.S. Eliot in his composition of *The Waste Land*.[11] This does not seem to me quite convincing. I would suggest that Woolf's novel and Eliot's poem share a pessimism which is partly a consequence of a similar response to European conditions which they experienced in common.

Woolf's view of life, then, has the universality of good art. It is also tragic. The tragic sense is generated partly by a general impression of life at Beddagama and life in general as a terrible struggle for existence. More importantly, the tragic sense is a consequence of the fates of his major characters. Silindu, Punchi Menika and Hinnihami enjoy only brief spells of happiness. For the most part, they experience miseries and their lives end pathetically. It is true that Silindu does not die at the close of the novel as do Punchi Menika and Hinnihami, but he is sentenced to twenty years' rigorous imprisonment and this is virtually death. The characters usually endure their miseries fatalistically, but Woolf himself does not endorse the fatalism. He suggests that their miseries are not a consequence of an external malignant Fate, but a matter of human responsibility. Silindu and Babun are victims of Babehami and Fernando not because of Fate, but because they are unequal to the cunning of the Headman and the urban trader. Silindu murders Babehami and Fernando because it was logical and just according to his primitive way of thinking ; he is responsible for his actions, not Fate. Similarly, it is in keeping with Punchi Menika's character that she remains and dies in Beddagama ; it is not a question of Fate. Hinnihami dies, not because of Fate, but because she herself lost the will to live ; she is unequal to life's problems. Thus, Woolf's novel conveys movingly a tragic theme, the cruelty of life and human frailty.

Yet tragedy is not ultimately depressing, nor is Woolf's novel. It has been argued by Yasmine Gooneratne and Stephen Medcalf that the novel offers certain positive values and that these values are Buddhist.[12] No doubt Silindu's meeting with the old beggar on the way to the Supreme Court session at Tangalle is important. It is through the old beggar that Woolf affirms certain Buddhist values, the value of meditation, the evil nature of all killing, the evil nature of desire and, indeed, the evil nature of life itself. In short, the beggar asserts the value of renouncing ordinary life. His preaching consoles Silindu, but it seems to me that Woolf's own acceptance of Buddhist values is qualified. The beggar condemns hunting as it is killing and thus continues his conversation with Silindu, the peon and other villagers :

> '......but what did the deer and pig do to you ? eh, hunter ? tell me that.' (says the old beggar)
>
> 'Do ? Nothing, of course. But there is no food up there. One must have food to live.' (says Silindu)
>
> 'No food up there ? There is always food upon the path, a handful of rice in every village, for the beggar. I have been forty years now on the path. Have I starved ?'
>
> 'What was your village, father ?'
>
> 'The name—I have forgotten—but it lay up there in the hills—a pleasant place—rain in plenty, and the little streams always running into the rice-fields, and cocoa-nut and areca-nut trees all around.'

> 'Ohe !' murmured one of the villagers, 'it is easy to avoid killing in a place like that.'
>
> 'Have you ever worked, old man ?' said the peon. 'Have you ever earned a fanam by work ? In this part of the country rupees don't grow on wara bushes.'
>
> 'No', said the old man ; 'I have never done anything like that. I am mad, you know. ......' (pp. 266-7).

Woolf suggests that Buddhist values have their attractiveness and logic and that, at the same time, these do not give one of the equipment to cope with ordinary life ; he suggests that society and life cannot continue if people generally followed the values propounded by the beggar.

Indeed, Woolf's criticism is implied, in the first place, by the very fact that the Buddhist values are put into the month of a person like the old beggar. Thus Woolf offers qualified positives in the form of Buddhist values. It also seems to me that there are other positives which are a more integral part of the action of the novel. Arnold Toynbee writes of *The Village in the Jungle* : "If the jungle is a malevolent beast of prey, then the villagers who have fought it with their bare hands are heroes whose story is an epic . . . . And when the jungle swallows up the village, we realize in retrospect that we have been reading a tale of human prowess which surpasses that tale told by the ruins of Angkor Wat."[13] I subscribe only partly to this interpretation of the novel ; Woolf conveys through his story of the villagers in the jungle a sense of the waste of human potentialities rather than a sense of heroism. Yet the hardihood and resilience of the villagers in grappling with their extremely difficult conditions of life are positive values. Equally important as positive values are the love and loyalty (in the face of cunning and grave hardship) embodied in the relationship of Punchi Menika and Babun.

7

A Passage to India seems to me one of the few great novels in the English language, like George Eliot's *Middlemarch* or Conrad's *Nostromo* or Lawrence's ***Women in Love***. I do not rate

The Village in the Jungle as high as Forster's masterpiece, certainly not higher than it as P.K. Elkin has done.[14] Woolf's presentation of social matters compares favourably with Forster's, but his novel has nothing equivalent to the metaphysical dimension of *A Passage to India*. I think that Forster successfully renders this metaphysical profundity: Mrs. Moore's character is a development from Mrs. Wilcox's in *Howards End*, but, unlike Mrs. Wilcox, she comes alive as both fully real and richly symbolic. *The Village in the Jungle* deserves to be recognised as a minor masterpiece, like Geogre Eliot's *Silas Marner*, a novel of a different kind but in the same class.

NOTES

1. E.M. Forster, *The Hill of Devi* (London : Penguin, 1965 ed.), pp. 153-4.
2. *The Village in the Jungle* was first published in 1913, reprinted twice in the same year, printed again in 1925 and 1931, and reprinted in the New Phoenix Library in 1951.
3. G. Jean-Aubry, *Joseph Conrad in the Congo* (Boston, 1926), p. 73.
4. Forster, op. cit., p. 10.
5. Leonard Woolf, *Growing: An Autobiography of the Years 1904—1911* (London : The Hogarth Press, 1964 ed.), p. 25.
6. Leonard Woolf, *The Village in the Jungle* (London : The Hogarth Press, 1961 ed.), p. 3 ; all later quotations from the novel are from this edition and their page-numbers are noted in my text.
7. P.K. Elkin, 'Leonard Woolf's Masterpiece' : *AUMLA, Journal of the Australasian Language and Literature Association*, No. 13, May 1960, p. 50.
8. Wordsworth, 'Preface' to *The Lyrical Ballads* (1800) : R.L. Brett and A.R. Jones (ed.), *Lyrical Ballads* (London : 1965 ed.), pp. 244-5.
9. Joyce Cary, 'Prefactory Essay' : *The African Witch* (London : Michael Joseph, 1961 ed.), p. 10.

10. "It is difficult to know why I found the jungle so fascinating. It is a cruel and dangerous place, and, being a cowardly person, I was always afraid of it".—Leonard Woolf, *Growing*, p. 211.

11. Yasmine Gooneratne, "Leonard Woolf's 'Waste Land' : *The Village in the Jungle*" : *The Journal of Commonwealth Literature*, Vol. 7, No. 1, June 1972, pp. 32-3.

12. Yasmine Gooneratne, op. cit., pp. 30-1 ; Stephen Medcalf, "*The Village in the Jungle*" ; *ADAM International Review*, Nos. 364-6, 1972, p. 77.

13. Arnold Toynbee, *A Study of History* (London : Oxford University Press, 1939 ed.), Vol. 2, p. 9.

14. P.K. Elkin, op. cit., p. 54.

———

CHAPTER 2

Lester James Peries' Village in the Jungle

Lester James Peries' film *Rekhāva* (1956) marked a decisive departure from South Indian cinematic tradition which had dominated the Sri Lankan scene and Peries went on to establish himself as the father of a distinctively Sinhalese cinema and win international recognition too. When a man of his stature makes a screen version of a distinguished novel such as Leonard Woolf's *The Village in the Jungle*, our expectations are great. He calls his film *Bäldegama*, the name of the village and also the title of the Sinhala translation of Woolf's novel.

Leonard Woolf who is known in the West as a political theorist and an active Labourite, a member of the Bloomsbury group and husband of Virginia, a publisher and the author of a highly acclaimed five-volume autobiography, worked in Ceylon from 1904 to 1911 as a civil servant when it was a crown colony and has a living reputation here as the author of *The Village in the Jungle*. The novel, reprinted last year by Oxford University Press, has been lauded by a few discerning foreigners such as Pablo Neruda, Arnold Toynbee, Kingsley Martin and Alec Waugh, but critics and the reading public in the West have paid it scant attention. I agree with majority Sri Lankan opinion that Woolf's novel is the finest creative work in English about our Island as does film-maker Peries who said : "Woolf's is the best novel written in English about Sri Lanka. In fact, it has no parallel in English writing about Asia—Woolf got closer than any other Western writer to the heart of Asian life."[1]

When the eagerly-awaited film appeared, it was greeted with howls of disappointment unmatched in Peries' career. It was condemned so roundly and almost universally that it was left to the director and his script-writer, A. J. Gunawardana, to defend it. But the fact is that the film has elicited a favourable response abroad, and Peries was driven to flaunt it as his trump card : 'How could the film be chosen as one of the 20 films out of 421 films for the Directors Fortnight at Cannes ? Why should it be chosen as one of the 20 films from around the world for this year's San Franciso Festival, if it was the cinematic disaster certain local critics said it was ? why should the committee of the London Film Festival select it this year, thereby guaranteeing it the accolade of being one of 1981's outstanding film achievements ? '[2] 'Are the professional, hard boiled critics and Festival Directors of Cannes, San Francisco, London, Toronto, Los Angeles, Arnhem, specialists who have devoted a lifetime to assessing movies guilty of a gross aberration of taste ? "[3] It has recently been reported that *Bäddegama* will be the first Sinhalese film to be screened over Channel 4 of the B.B.C. which was launched in 1982.

It seems to me that both these diametrically opposed responses are valid and relevant to a consideration of the total value of the film and, taken together, suggest a way of gaining an all-sided view of the film.

I share the view of local critics who felt that the film fell far short of the book in its quality, impact and significance, bearing in mind the differences in media. The director and script-writer, in their desperate defence, insisted that the expectations raised by the book were irrelevant and presumptuous when evaluating the film as a film, but their stand is hardly tenable when they have openly acknowledged that they were engaged in translating the novel into cinematic terms and Peries even said : "Of course neither A.J. nor I had ever intended perpetrating any infidelities on Woolf's celebrated book. After all hadn't I waited 10 long patient years to obtain the rights to film the movie ? "[4]

At the same time, I think the film-makers have a right to do whatever they please with the book to suit their own ends and the film must, in the end, be judged as a film independently of the book.

A.J. Gunawardana has referred to "the structures of exploitation (economic, bureaucratic, legal) dramatised in the film"[5] and there are scenes of the traders of the town taking away the produce of villagers as repayment for loans and of the miscarriage of justice but it seems to me that, unlike the book, the film does not gather up the life of the whole community of peasants into its course and is essentially a family drama of Silindu the father, his twin daughters Punchi Menika and Hinnihami, their aunt Karlinahami who looked after them because their mother died at childbirth, and, later, Punchi Menika's husband Babun. While thus narrowing drastically the scope of the book, the film both simplifies and glamorizes the family drama itself. In the film, Silindu constantly carries a gun and his gun is the only evidence that he is a hunter, but in the book this side of his character was fully rendered and there were more aspects to it : he both loved the jungle and feared it, while being at the same time at home in it. In the book, his daughters were healthier and more attractive than the other villagers but, in the film, they were positively glamorous and over-nourished and have none of the 'wildness and strangeness' which, in the book, they have and which are a part of Silindu's own character. Babun, the brother-in-law of the village headman, Babehami, falls in love with Punchi Menika. An opening shot shows Babun, from a distance and hiding behind a tree, admiring Punchi Menika who is bathing at the village tank—a stereotyped romatic shot which has no basis in the book and is quite alien to its spirit. Soon after Babun takes Punchi Menika to him, at first by force and later by consent. Babun ripping off Punchi Menika's blouse is the typical primitive he-man, dear to conventional sophisticated taste, and his mating with Punchi Menika is not the perfectly natural event it is in the book.

In its attempt to cater to mass Westernized taste, the film stresses sex and dwells on those episodes of the book which lend themselves to such treatment—on Punchirala, the village medicine man, as he lusts after Punchi Menika's sister, Hinnihami, though spurned by both Hinnihami and Silindu ; on Fernando, the cunning urban trader who comes to the village to collect his debts, as he lusts after Punchi Menika and tries in vain to shake the loyalty of Babun and Punchi Menika to each other. The film also ministers to the sense of exoticism of the conventionally sophisticated. When Silindu believes that Punchirala, angered by his opposition to Punchirala's marriage proposal has induced devils to take possession of him, his mental state is conveyed with this kind of crudeness : Silindu sees devil masks, peddled to tourists, appearing in and out of the trees around him. Again, when Silindu's family take him on a pilgrimage to the shrine of God Kataragama to exercise the devils in him, the entire ritual is a caricature of the real.

It is in keeping with its commercial slant and dynamics that the film exploits violence and ends with two murders. When Hinnihami treats a fawn as if it were her child, the villagers condemn both as evil and attack them in a prolonged gory and sensational episode. At the conclusion of the film, Silindu suddenly understands that Fernando and Babehami, the village headman, are responsible for creating problems for him and shoots them as a primitive man's method of getting rid of his tormentors. In the film, Silindu appears a mumbling idiot with a gun, a potential murderer from the start, but in the book his understanding of his enemies is reached as hard-won wisdom after stomaching a series of misfortunes. The film has no place for episodes after the murders which are in the book—such as Silindu's meeting with an old Buddhist beggar on his way to prison, an important meeting from which he derives consolation and through which Leonard Woolfs affirms the qualified value of Buddhist precepts.

The film is a family drama of sex, intrigue and revenge. It has no consistent focus or thread. Lester James Peries said : 'There are, if one breaks up the narrative line, 4 different stories in the novel and they are held together primarily by Woolf's style. '[6] While disagreeing with Peries' notion of the novel's complicatedness—if Woolf's novel can be broken up into four different stories, George Eliot's *Middlemarch* can be broken up into over a hundred, I think Woolf's novel is also held together by Silindu's finely portrayed character. He was not a mindless hunter as in the film, but a human being, sensitive, capable of changing and developing, having a sense of values which is tellingly demonstrated when he resolutely supports Punchi Menika's rejection of Fernando.

In addition, the book was unified by the constant presence of the threatening jungle which gradually swallows up the entire village. There are lingering shots of a writhing snake and a full-grown leopard but these seem an exhibition as in a zoo for the Westernised audience, and the film does not catch the real menace and overhanging presence of the jungle. In fact, the setting seems far too green and lush whereas, according to the book, this should have happened only during a highly exceptional season. The film thus misses an important part of the book's meaning and certain positive values it affirms : the book shows the hardihood and resilience of the disease-stricken villagers as they wrest a living out of an arid, inhospitable jungle land.

The whole environment, the entire action, characters and situations in the film seem sufficiently presentable so that a Westernized audience would not recoil in horror, yet are shown up as primitive so as to pander to or create a sense of superiority in them—an approach quite alien to the book. The villagers in the book have a sense of values and win our respect for the ways in which they cope with their problems. I would venture to suggest that the values of the Westernized audience of the film may seem shoddy in comparison with theirs.

The very nature of the film lends itself to the opposed reactions of the local critics and Western audiences. Leonard Woolf's novel is rather simple and its technique so strongly visual that I feel it would not have been difficult to make a realistic, serious and richly meaningful film out of it. I remember how well D.H. Lawrence's far more difficult novel, *Women in Love*, was transmuted in the film with Alan Bates, Glenda Jackson and Oliver Reed. If the Sri Lankan film-makers deliberately emasculated Woolf's book to cater to mass Westernized and Western stereotypes and if at the same time they were trying to cash in on the novel's local reputation, then the film has no artistic integrity. If they were unconscious that they were in fact doing so, then they have failed to make the journey to Beddegama from Colombo which Woolf did from Bloomsbury.

NOTES

1. A.J. Gunawardana, 'The Village in the Jungle' : *Sight and Sound*, Vol. 49, No. 1, Winter 1979/80, p. 26.
2. Lester James Peries, 'Novel into Film' : *Lanka Guardian*, Vol. 4, No. 11, 1 October, 1981, p. 13.
3. Lester James Peries, 'Critics in the Jungle' : *Lanka Guardian*, Vol. 4, No. 13, 15 November 1981, p. 13.
4. Lester James Peries, 'Novel into Film' : *Lanka Guardian*, Vol. 4, No. 11, October 1981, p. 12.
5. A.J. Gunawardana, 'Cinema and Commitment' : *Lanka Guardian*, Vol. 4, No. 13, 15 November, 1981, p. 15.
6. Peries, 'Novel in to Film' : *Lanka Guardian*, Vol. 4, No. 11, 1 October, 1981, p. 13.

CHAPTER 3

Language planning in Sri Lanka

Language planning as a part of socio-linguistic study came into being in the late 1960s and it arrived on the scene too late for Sri Lanka to benefit fully from its insight because crucial language changes in Sri Lanka occurred in the late 1950s. In 1956, when Sinhalese displaced English as the national and official language as well as the medium of instruction in secondary schools and, later, universities for the Sinhalese, the linguistic situation was complex and tense. There was a common form of colloquial Sinhalese recognized by ordinary speakers of the language together with regional variations and a standard form of written Sinhalese accepted by the literate, leaving aside a tiny minority arguing for "pure" Sinhalese. The new responsibilities of Sinhalese entailed pressures towards overall standardisation and modernization and there was conflict between the younger writers who favoured colloquial Sinhalese and the scholars who inclined towards literary Sinhalese. An Official Languages Department was set up partly to modernize Sinhalese, and the modernization was carried out partly by this Department and partly by enterprising scholars. The battle between the younger writers and the scholars has become more complicated with the battle-lines being crossed. Tamil, the language of the minority community, was permitted to be used by its speakers in all their dealings, was the medium of instruction for Tamils and had a common spoken form with regional variations and a standard written form recognized by the entire community. Tamil had the advantage of being developed in South India, whereas Sinhalese is a language of Sri Lanka alone and had to be developed here alone.

English, an established language, need not be planned in its native-speaker context in Britain and as an international language, but needs to be planned in its form and role in each foreign country that wishes to use it. It is the latter, in its Sri Lankan context, that concerns me here.

I. The socio-political context of English

When Sri Lanka needed an international auxiliary language, English automatically slipped into this position because of historical circumstances: she had been a British colony since 1976. But English was not automatically accorded this position. In the wake of the nationalistic fervours of 1956, understandably but regrettably, English was extruded and excluded from a position of importance; it was neglected for thirty years and a whole generation suffered. Sri Lanka needed, and still needs. *English as an international language* for several reasons: to have access to world knowledge, especially in science and technology; to move into the computer age; and to engange in international trade and commerce, diplomacy, international relations in general. Sri Lanka also needs *English as an intra-language*. English has to be promoted nationally for at least three reasons: to serve as a "link language", to develop a cohesive multi-cultural society; to serve as a means of bridging the generation gap (if one simplifies Sri Lankan society as consisting of speakers of Sinhalese, speakers of Tamil and an older generation of English speakers, including both Sinhalese and Tamils, English could be the bridge between the first two groups and the last); and to provide equality of opportunity in a country where English is still the preserve of a privileged minority. The encouragement of English is a politically sensitive issue: it could be construed as belittling and harming Sinhalese, and could be so exploited by political opponents. The attitudes of society to English are complicated: everybody wants to know English for a variety of reasons (for prestige, even for the sake of snobbery as well as for enhancement of personality and its utilitarian value in education and in securing employment) but those who do not know it, hate those who do. Thus society maintains a kind of love-hate relationship with English.

II. The variety of English to be used

It is usually a problem for former British colonies to choose the variety of English it is going to teach in schools and universities. Singapore, faced with a choice between Singaporean English and Standard English, opted for Standard English, but in Sri Lanka the problem is not acute. Professor Thiru Kandiah argues that Lankan English is "an independent, distinctive and fully formed linguistic system adequate for the communicative and expressive needs of its users"[1] but, while granting that he has a case, I think he has made too much of the differences between Sri Lankan English and Standard English. Sri Lankan English has evolved its own distinctive characteristics of phonology, idiom, vocabulary and grammar which are completely intelligible in its social context, but the English speaking community in Sri Lanka does not seem to me sufficiently large and independent-minded to be capable of evolving a dialect like Australian English. In fact, Standard Sri Lankan English speech, though it differs from Standard English, is not widely so and is intelligible to speakers of Standard English. In writing, Standard Sri Lankan English is even closer to Standard English and the difference is negligible. Therefore, Sri Lanka has chosen almost as a matter of course to teach Standard Sri Lankan English in its schools and universities and I would argue that there is no need to play up its differences from Standard English.

III. The extent and duration of support to be given to learners of English

(a) School education

The first question is how early the learning of English should begin in schools. The present system whereby English-learning begins at grade three, can be justified on financial grounds (funds do not permit learning beginning earlier) and on the grounds of maldistribution of teachers (there are insufficient teachers in rural schools to start the programme earlier) but not necessarily on grounds of language ecquisition. It is commonly argued that it is better to consolidate learning the first language before learning the second but this is not necessarily true as was borne out by research in Philippines in this field in the 1960s.[2] However, one cannot be definite because our knowledge of early bilingualism is insufficient. On the other hand, if we begin teaching English at grade one in schools in which teachers are available, one has to contend with a fresh set of problems. Would not this provision give pupils in these schools an unfair advantage in the field of education and, later, employment? The government, if it sticks to its commitment to provide text books, will have to issue a new series of books. Young language learners learn quickly but, if the teacher is bad, they will be adversely affected for a long time. If the teachers recent teaching from grade one and dislike their job, they will communicate this to their pupils.

The second question is to whom should English be taught. It is possible to argue that English should be taught to all pupils because there is an important educational value in the intellectual activity entailed in language learning. But the fact is that not all pupils will need English. Is it possible to choose, at an early age, those pupils who will need and benefit from English? Has anyone the right to choose for a child whose future is unknown? How can we make provision for those who develop late in life ? Rural children will not need English if they remain in villages, but if we were to stop teaching them English, we would restrict social mobility and employment opportunities. Is it right not to equip rural children with English which will be useful if they migrate to the towns? But can a small country with scarce resources afford to finance an all-embracing programme of English teaching? Is such an investment worth while? The questions are numerous but it is to practical considerations that we must pay head, In the 1970s, Thailand tried the experiment of making English optional, but it failed; competition is rife in society; if some students genuinely wish to learn English and opt for it, others fellow suit; if one student knows English, others want to learn it too. The Government will have to decide to whom it is going to teach English, leaving out students from the decision-making process, but this may raise political problems. A fair solution is possible when a country reaches the stage where good teachers of English are available in all the schools, both urban and rural. Then, a Government can offer English-teaching during primary school and allow only those who perform well in the language, to proceed in their studies in this field. Students of English in secondary school are thereby chosen by a process of self selection. Yet this process is expensive.

English is particularly needed by Sri Lankan students who wish to pursue higher education, but it is not tested after the

G.C.E. (Ordinary Level) Examination. Consequently given perfectly normal student psychology, there is a lack of motivation to learn the language and even no English-teaching after O/L in some schools. There is a dire need for a General English paper (apart from English as a subject) at the G.C.E. (Advanced Level) Examination which should be made compulsory for all candidates to sit and, when there are sufficient English teachers in all schools, compulsory for all candidates to pass if they wish to be admitted to the universities. A target and time-frame and a programme for this purpose must be formulated as a matter of urgency. Moreover, in a country where only about 5,000 are admitted to universities out of 30,000 who qualify for admission, a General English programme in A/L classes would equip students to follow training programmes and acquire skills outside the universities and enable them to find employment, a valuable opening particularly for those who are unable to enter the universities. Of course, whether the state should provide university education for all those who satisfy the basic requirements is a related question and even though it may be theoretically desirable, it will involve such practical problems as employment of more graduates.

The third issue is the objective of English teaching in the schools. In Sri Lanka, for the last ten years or so, the objective has been reading comprehension and it has vitiated out ESI programme. From the point of view of acquisition of knowledge and culture, reading comprehension seems a perfectly adequate aim and, among the four skills, only reading and writing can be assessed with fairness, particularly so if large numbers have to be tested. Reading comprehension provides a basis for assessment but is, certainly, not a method of teaching. Even reading comprehension has to be taught with the aid of the other skills. The skills reinforce each other and the methodology of ELT thereby improves. Whatever one's objective is, it is best to teach a combination of skills, and adopt an integrated approach to language teaching. Moreover, all four skills are needed for the development of personality and for certain kinds of employment, particularly in the private sector.

(b) English at the University

The universities have to mount ESL programmes because the programme in schools is very much a failure. One can readily understand Sri Lanka's plight if one compares it with Singapore's: the National University of Singapore finds it necessary to teach remedial English to a significant proportion of students whose medium of instruction in schools has been English. In Nigeria, especially in the North, students who have been taught English for 10 years in schools and who have studied all their subjects in English, have to be taught remedial English in universities. Even in the United States of America, a significant number of undergraduates who are native speakers of the language, have to be taught remedial English. Until the ESL programme in Sri Lankan school is improved—a stupendous task, ESL instruction in the universities will have to continue.

Sri Lanka seems to have realised, though no one in authority has explicitly stated the matter, that it is impossible to keep pace with advancing knowledge through translations in the local languages. The main aim of the ESL programmes in the universities is to equip the students to acquire knowledge and the emphasis is on reading comprehension, though study skills are important. Thus it is logical to teach English for special purposes. But teaching ESP has proved more difficult than general language teaching. The teacher of ESP has to know English as well as the subjects of students and such teachers are hard to come by. The choice of materials for ESP teaching is not easy and the English teacher may have to sit in on lectures in the subjects of the students and, certainly, have to cansult the subject lecturers. But, in practice, in Sri Lanka the problems are even more complicated. General English too has to be taught, if the ESL courses are to equip students to students to find employment, to develop personality and to benefit from the media. Moreover, the most pressing demand of students is for teaching speech and what may be called "social English" so that they can gain a status in society. It is extremely difficult to reconcile these objectives and demands, and structure courses within the limited time available for language teaching. The pre-university Intensive Course in English—an eight-week course conducted during the long vacation just prior to new entrants beginning their undergraduate studies—is of immense use, but the ideal solution would be for General English to be taught effectively in the schools and for the universities to build ESP courses upon that foundation. Of course, the still more ideal solution would be for ESL programmes in the schools to be so successful that there will be no need for such courses at universities!

Asmah Haji Omar has noted the prerequisites of a university proficiency course in English:

(a) effective teaching
(b) sound teaching methods
(c) suitable teaching materials[3]

The far more difficult task is to discover what actually constitutes these items.

Those of us who supervise ESL course at universities have to contend with a problem that crops up every year—the flagging of student interest and motivation when the examinations in their main subjects draw close. This tendency is encouraged by the fact that they have seen fellow students perform well without knowing English. To call this an intellectual heresy on the part of examiners is not to put things too strongly; examiners should demand reading outside lecture notes. The situation could be remedied by making a pass in English language at elementary level a compulsory degree requirement. I suggest a pass only at elementary level so as to be fair by undergraduates who have been educated in rural and less privileged schools and whose grasp of English is so poor at admission that they cannot be expected to proceed to an advanced level within time allotted for language teaching. It will be possible to impose more stringent requirements when the programme in schools more effective and better organised.

IV. Teacher problems

I see three important problems relating to teachers in the ESL programme in schools. First, the maldistribution of teachers. The lack of teachers in rural schools is due not to insufficient numbers but to unequal distribution As English teachers are part of a Government service, it is possible for a Government to compel teachers to work in rural areas for a certain period. A significant proportion of English teachers are women and are married, and they do not wish to leave their husbands who, more often than not, work in towns. In such cases, it will be necessary for the Government to formulate a scheme at a high level and, where possible, transfer both husband and wife to the same rural area for a time. But it is nothing but fair to provide facilities and incentives to those who work in 'difficult' areas. Housing is a necessity. Estate labourers are provided housing, don't the teachers deserve it ? Such teachers should be given salary increments and preference when selections are made for training and study at home and abroad. To meet the immediate need of the lack of teachers in rural areas it would be useful to offer appointments on contract to retired teachers to serve in these areas. Even retired government servants and mercantile employees, educated in English, may be pressed into service.

The second problem is that of ill-qualified teachers. Large numbers of G.C.E. O/L qualified personnel have been recruited into the teaching service when a pass in O/L English certifies very little, given the present requirements for a pass, certainly not competent in the language. Such teachers are in dire need of in-service training courses in language such as the Key English Language Teaching Instiute is trying to provide but cannot cope with the numbers in need of such courses.

The third problem is that of ill-trained teachers. The curricula of training-colleges have too many subjects unrelated to ELT even Hygiene, Physical Education and Agriculture, and should concentrate on ELT. Trainees begin to study their subjects immediately after admission, whereas most of them are so weak in their English language that the colleges would do better to conduct an intensive course in the language for the first three months, if not longer. In fact, I would suggest that a pass in the intensive course in the language be made a condition for admission to teacher-training.

V. Central Language Planning Agency

At present, ESL course in schools are plannned by the English unit of the Ministry of Education. It has done a great deal of work, but has not been sufficiently successful. I suggest that language planning be moved away from the Ministry of Education and the Government set up a Central Language Planning Agency for all three language, English, Sinhalese and Tamil. Personnel from the English Unit could be absorbed into the new Agency but they need not form its nucleus, perhaps better not if the new Agency is to start afresh and think afresh. The key personnel in the new Agency should be more qualified and deeply versed in language teaching. The ideal function of the new Agency would be to give advice to the government during the actual formulation of an integrated language policy; to refine, interpret and help to explain the policy once it has been formulated; to plan the implementation of various aspects of the policy or advise other agencies and institutions on implementation strategies (this may include surveys, pilot projects and the like); to conduct or monitor some implementation activities directly and advice the other agencies and institutions that conduct or monitor them; to evaluate all planning or implementation activities, whether conducted by the central language agency or not and to evaluate the policy itself and recommend to government changes in the policy as needed. The ideal organizational model of the Agency would be for it to enjoy a status equivalent to agencies or boards that advise the government on political, military, economic and scientific matters; not to be attached to any Ministry, but report directly to the prime Minister or President; to be a permanent agency, with career positions and control of own budget; and to have authority to contract for additional services from the public and private sectors and the universities as needed.

NOTES

1. Thiru Kandiah, 'Disinherited Englishes : the case of Lankan English' : *Navasilu* Vol. IV, 1981, p. 102.

2. Fredrick B. Davis, *Philippine Language—Teaching Experiments* (Quezon City : Alemar-Phoenix Publishing House, 1967), pp. iv-v.

3. Asmah Haji Omar, *The Teaching of Bahasa Malaysia in the Context of National Language Planning* (Kuala Lumpur: Dewan Bahasa Dan Pustaka Kementarian Pelajaran Malaysia 1976), p. 114.

4. I wish to thank Dr. Richard Noss for discussing these points with me. It is to him that I owe my ideas on the functions and organization of a central language planning agency. All shortcomings are my own.

I first began to think systematically about Language Planning when I was a member of the English Language Committee of Inquiry appointed by the Minister of Education during 1980-81 and I have benefited from its deliberations.

CHAPTER 4

Beyond Alienation : The Efflorescence of Sri Lankan Literature in English

I have not chosen The English Language, it has chosen me.

—Joseph Conrad

In their survey of contemporary Sri Lankan literature in English, Ariya Abeysinghe and Iranganie Abeysinghe judged that it 'has shown more promise than fulfilment.'[1] That was in 1970. Is their assessment valid today, more than a decade later, as it was then ?

As in many ex-colonial countries, the colonial period in Sri Lanka's history was, despite fitful flashes, generally a dark period as far as original writing in English by 'natives' was concerned; it did produce the novel *The Village in the Jungle* (1913), still the finest imaginative work about the island, but that was by an Englishman, Leonard Woolf, just as the best creative work in English in the 19th century, *Forest Life in Ceylon* (1854), was by another Englishman, William Knighton. The presence of the colonial masters had a suffocating impact on the creative potential of the local inhabitants and it was only after Independence (1948) that a body of literature in English by Sri Lankans began to emerge. Actually, this had to wait till the 1960s. Sri Lanka was granted Independence by Britain partly as a consequence of the freedom struggle in India and, partly because our Independence was won comparatively more easily, in fact, too easily, Sri Lankans had not forged as strong as national consciouness as the Indians. Even after 1948, the ruling and social elites consisted of, 'brown sahibs'. But it did not take long for nationalist currents to surface, however extremist they might have been, and 1956 is, in several ways, a watershed in Sri Lankan history. Symbolically speaking, a national dress replaced top hat and coat tails and English was displaced from its pre-eminent position as the official language and the medium of instruction in schools and universities. English had to be relegated to the status of a second language, sooner or later, despite the regrets of the English-educated privileged classes, but it was not properly treated as such; it was neglected for, at least, two decades and even reviled. Paradoxically, it was in this context that literature in English came into prominence : national and creative instincts run deeper than problems of language and class.

The immediate problem faced by writers in English was that, while indigenous blood flowed in their veins and indigenous or personal concerns prompted them to write creatively, they were alienated from the mass of the people by virtue of their English affiliations. Their predicament is partly illustrated by Ashley Halpé's poem 'The Boyhood of Chittha', a sensitive account of, and a reaction to, his upbringing under the influence of two cultures. He first imbibes his native culture in the form of stories of old, which blend history and legend :

Gemunu, tearing out brilliant ear-rings
for the starved monk, reeked copious blood
on golden shoulder-blades; his famous elephant
was huge as a double-decker, wise as father;
and Yesodhara blushed in every breeze,
so fine her noble skin.

His kind of progress is towards Western culture which moulds his early poetry :

And so to Robin Hood, Drake-filled Devon,
Prince Arthur, and Lancelot of the Lake,
(Abridged and Simplified). At Seven
he versified—after a fashion—
Horatius, Columbus, the evening star.

Significantly, he learnt of his own culture from a servant who, moreover, 'not surprisingly, was sacked', and he controls his bitterness towards both the circumstances into which he was born and his own divided personality. Given this kind of conditioning, it came naturally to a poet in the 1960s, Gamini Seneviratne, to write of his personal predicament in this vein in 'Two Songs of Myself':

> Am a lone wolf
> In the winter forest gnawing
> the ice
> If I should see a man
> Stamping into warmth on covered thighs
> I'd pull him down
> And tear at him........

It is not illegitimate for a poet to use culturally alien (in this instance, extended) imagery. The poet has the right to exploit every area of experience and every resource of language, alien or not, and this kind of Western experience and language may even be regarded as having become international through common knowledge and currency. In a way, the crucial question is whether the poet communicates his meaning and, in this case, Seneviratne, certainly, does so on his own rather adolescent level. But all this is less than complete justification and *how well* he conveys his meaning is an important question : that Seneviratne should write in this manner is evidence of his deracination and his style is thereby less immediate.

The English language was taken for granted by many writers in Sri Lanka but, in others, it excited strong feelings and even contributed to dislocating personality. In 1965, Lakdasa Wikkramasinha wrote :

> I have come to realise that I am using the language of the most despicable and loathsome people on earth; I have no wish to extend its life and range, enrich its tonality.
>
> To write in English is a form of cultural treason. I have had for the future to think of a way of circumventing this treason; I propose to do this by making my writing entirely immoralist and destructive.[2]

It is partly his reaction to his English affiliations that makes Wikkramasinha a radical. He spells out his credo in 'The Poet':

> He is the one that, tossing a bomb into
> The crowd, takes notes;

The one who, from an unseen distance
Levels on the tripod that black rifle
With sights that see as far as his soul
Trains and levels, manoeuvres for a clear sight
Of the speaker on the plateform;
Waits, watching the clock, for the onset of a car
In the left corner of its back seat
Carrying the enemy.
The poet is the one who is always preparing
The ambush, the one who
Covers with layers of
Earth and grass and worn wood,
The spiked pit,
And watches from the level of woods ahead;
The poet is the bomb in the city,
Unable to bear the circle of the
Seconds in his heart,
Waiting to burst.

The imagery is rich, genuinely surprising and contemporaneous. The images do not flow one into the other but they all cohere under the general banner of the poet as a rebel with a social and political consciousness. Notwithstanding Wikkramasinha's self-posturing, the poem has an impact and helps us to understand Wikkramasinha and others of his ilk. But Wikkramasinha had an aristocratic ancestry and, while his compassion would flow towards the underprivileged in society as, for example, the servant girl exploited sexually an otherwise in 'The Death of Ashanthi', an ingrained aristocratic streak remains, suggested, for instance, by the fulsome praise accorded the feudal lady in 'From the Life of the Folk-poet Ysinno' :

Then the kind Menike said, O then
You take what straw you need from the behind shed.
And Ysinno being a folk-poet, and his lines being not all dead,
The benison of the Menike of Iddamalgoda
Lives even today.

Wikkramasinha's, then, is not an integrated personality and it is from the tensions within him that his poetry and its vitality spring. He was conscious of his own worth as a poet : this lies behind the cheap humour he levels at the Professor in 'Work of a Professor', a deterioration of the satirical stance in better poems :

What does the Professor do ?
He plants brinjals
all day because he's too
intelligent
to do anything else.
But he loves his country;
he loves poetry . . .
—and so the Professor
with his brass
forehead, and his quick and sure.
voice, keeps telling me, you'll
never be
'known'.

Wikkramasinha perhaps overestimated himself as a poet, but this sense of his worth, together with an undaunted fortitude in the face of a discouragingly small reading public, motivated him, like Peter Scharen, another notable Sri Lankan poet now settled in Australia, to keep on publishing privately slim volumes of poetry. Wikkramasinha's achievement in that among our poets his is 'the most distinctive voice' and that 'his is the poetry most consistently Ceylonese in its material'[3] has been noticed time and again, and he succeeded in making a virtue of his problems, but he died ere his prime, leaving behind a small body of work of interest both sociologically and poetically yet without suggesting in what directions his undoubted talent may have developed.

Unlike Lakdasa Wikkramasinha, Yasmine Gooneratne takes to the English language without trauma and even approaches it as a lover in her poem 'This Language, This woman' :

So do not call her slut, and alien,
names born of envy and your own misuse
that whisper how desire in secret runs.
She has known greatness, borne illustrious sons,
her mind's well-stored, her lovely nature's rich,
filled with these splendid warm surprises which,

now the distorting old connection's done,
fit her to be your mistress, and my Muse.

She masters an alien language and alien forms in her poetry with no problems being caused by their alienness, and perhaps her greatest gift is her ability to think in images, especially when she transcends the Westernized upper class to which she belongs (this, incidentally, helps her to feel at home in alien or Western matters). In 'Peace-Game', she does so and satirically and allegorically contemplates class conflict; the pressure of the poetry is such that it suggests another dimension, international power politics too :

We Evens were a well-fed lot
and tough, so that the little patched
and scrawny Odds would never dare
to say the teams were not well matched.
That was the beauty of the game,
we chose the ground and made the rules,
they couldn't really do a thing
about it, stunted little fools,
Except to put quite a fight
sometimes, against our guns and such.
We called the entertainment 'Peace'
or 'War'—I can't remember which . . .

Satire, while it could deteriorate into vituperation and spite even in her most ambitious poem, *The Lizard's Cry*, is her strength, yet she is capable of combining it with deep feeling as in 'Words to a Daughter' and writing effective love poetry too as in 'Rocks on Marine Drive' and 'White Cranes'.

While in Sri Lanka, alienation though it prevented Yasmine Gooneratne from tuning on to the wave-length of the mass of the people and limited her range, did not staunch her creativity, but she was driven to emigrate to Australia, probably partly because of 'the solemn dons and grave administrators' she satirises in 'Masks in the University Senate Room' (she was a Lecturer in English at the University of Peradeniya), and experiences a kind of alienation different from the writer in Sri Lanka. Her first collection of poems *World, Bird, Motif* appeared in 1971, her second *The Lizard's Cry* in 1972, while *6000 Ft Death Dive* contains poems written in Australia, Honolulu and Sri Lanka between 1972 and 1981, nine years for a slim volume of 29 short poems, a performance disappointing for a poet so prolific earlier and explicable in terms of her emigration as portrayed in the poems themselves. She is still capable of writing warmly on the theme of love, while an academic of the University of Peradeniya rouses her wrath as of old, but Australia has diminished her satiric fire and wrought changes. Lakshmi de Silva has noticed a new tendency in her technique : 'It is as though the clarity and predictable precision of her earlier style has ceased to satisfy her and she is now exploring the resources of resonance, the depths and echose that rim the edge of a poet's line.'[4] More significant, however, is her new preoccupation with exile, the main subject of the volume, especially the difficulty and the writing of poetry in Australia. Like Coleridge in the 'Ode on Dejection,' Yasmine Gooneratne in her new vein is communicating about an inability to communicate. Her position as an alienated emigrant is, I think, responsible for the poetry in this volume not quite achieving the quality of her earlier verse.

Patrick Fernando's poetry is not deeply rooted in Sri Lanka as that of Lakdasa Wikkramasinha or, to a lesser extent, of Yasmine Gooneratne, and he copes with the problem of alienation by often retreating into a personal world and minimising it by his kinship with the world of the Classics and Christianity which play an important role in his poetry. His language is of polished, his forms so well crafted and also orthodox, and his poetic world often non-specific that my university students often mistake him for a British poet in my practical criticism classes. 'Chorus on a Marriage' reveals him at his characteristic best. He contemplates the decline of feelings in a human relationship in terms of an allegorical framework of the vicissitudes in a kingdom resulting from the death of successive rulers :

Swiftly their love sickened, and patiently,
Without one murmur, in a year or two,
Departed. The grave was dug in memory.

A faint awareness stood as monument.
No epitaph except the world's wild guess :
The wise observed a searing of the will,
The pious blamed a lack of timely grace,
While cynics certified love mortal. Still,
How magnificent love's coronation—
The virtues all attending, all princes present,
And roads dizzy with dancing !
So limited a reign forecast by none.

The couple are not particularised and this facilitates a general application of the poet's theme. The incongruity between the elevatedness of the allegorical framework the imagery, and the ordinariness of the human realities generates a satirical tone and reveals the satirical standpoint of the poet which both controls and inhibits the feelings of pathos. The poem descends briefly from fantasy to the real world in the last stanza :

He scans the share list, chuckling now and then,
And she is knitting socks for charities,
Both dreaming of a girl known long ago.

The scene is conventional, Western, not Sri Lankan, and mars the poem slightly.

Sri Lanka's English poets have coped with the problem of alienation in diverse ways and have succeeded in writing notable poems which, though they, inevitably, fall short of the output of more populous excolonies with more English-speakers like India, compare favourably in quality with good poetry anywhere. The novelists have coped with the same problem but with somewhat less success. Though English-educated and urban-based, they have often set their novels and stories in the countryside or deal with rural characters as though they can thereby present truly national, authentically Sri Lankan experiences and find roots in the soil. Thus, though urban-rural dichotomy in James Goonewardene's novels conforms to the traditions Raymond Williams saw in England and which are, probably, universal—

On the country has gathered the idea of a natural way of life : of peace, innocence and simple virtue. On the city has gathered the idea of an achieved centre : of learning communi-

> cation, light. Powerful, hostile associations have also developed : on the city as a place of noise, worldliness, and ambition ; on the country as a place of backwardness, ignorance, limitation.[5]—

it is complicated by his position as an alienated writer in English in Sri Lanka and strengthened by common sense : in *A Quiet Place*, the hero, Abhaya, a victim of *ennui* and disappointed in the love of an urban 'respectable' woman, seeks peace and contentment in a village, yet 'came to realise that the village, no less than the city was full of cant and hypocrisy.'[6] Abhaya wins the affection of Nandini, an embodiment of rural virtues, and battles valiantly against his enemies who even induce the superstitious villagers to believe that the prevalent drought was caused by the pollution wrought by the urban outsider. The rains too come in the nick of time to aid Abhaya but the conclusion does not seem an entirely facile happy ending because it suggests that Abhaya's success in the future is not fully assured. Although conceptually the novel is fairly complex and interesting, the ideas are not worked out in rich and substantial fictional terms, though *A Quiet Place* is certainly less simplistic than *Call of the Kirala.*

Punyakante Wijenaike is more interested than James Goonewardene in the countryside in its own right, as evident in many of the stories of her first work *The Third Woman,* and her first novel, *The Waiting Earth. The Third Woman* is still her finest work and, though she is guilty of minor lapses as when she writes 'It was a good harvest with the full ripe stalks standing proudly in the sun'[7] (the full ripe paddy stalks usually bend under their weight), her portrayal of rural life is splendidly realistic. It permits her, in her iitle story, to convey powerfully a theme of unmotivated evil as one of Diyonis Baas' mistresses proceeds to murder the others, while the loose domestic relations depicted in the story have an actual social basis in the 'upcountry' areas of Sri Lanka. In 'The Promise', a soothsayer promises that the gods will grant Isohamy a new house in place of her 'half-tumbled down little shack' and she believes his explanation when the prophecy was not fulfilled :

> 'When I put your request forward apparently the God in charge of granting favours had been away an a holiday and a

> subordinate was acting. This lesser God, without consulting his superior, rashly promised a house within a month's time. When the great one returned he was angry....'[8]

Thus, Punyakante Wijenaike exposes a kind of gullibility as well as cunning common among the peasantry.

She tries to get to grips more directly with the problem of alienation when she contemplates the class to which she belongs, the upper class, in her third work, a *nouvelle, Giraya.* Adeline, the widowed head of an aristocratic great house, her very name, an Anglicised one, a sign of her alienation, rules the house with an iron hand. The whole upper-class way of life is shown to be decadent to the point of corruption and it is recorded in a diary kept by a victim of that life, Kamini, the outsider, the Sinhalese-speaking, Sinhalese-educated, wife of Adeline's son, Lal. Kamini's education and sensitivity emerge as positive values in an otherwise negative novel and she represents the normal which is employed as a criticism of the upper class. Punyakante Wijenaike, in fact, seems to be turning against her own class, in the novel. Its denouement is melodramatic but throws an interesting light on the author. Too many sensational things happen : Adeline is murdered and the crazy old family retainer Lucia Hamy commits suicide ; Adeline herself is shown to be immoral, Lal being an illegitimate child of hers ; Lal turns out to be a homosexual, while her daughter, Manel, has been engaged in a clandestine love affair with the Superintendent of her estate. Though these events and disclosures illuminate the earlier behaviour of these characters, they are not really woven into the body of the action so as to enrich it and thereby there is a certain thinness in the articulation of the themes. More importantly, these things suggest that the author is suffering from a sense of guilt (in relation to her social group) which intensifies into a kind of paroxysm at the close. Having expiated her guilt in fictional terms, Punyakante Wijenaike was ready to deal with public drama, the insurgency of 1971, in her next major work, another *nouvelle, The Rebel.*

The insurgency in 1971 was the only planned and mass uprising since Independence against parliamentary government. It was confined mainly to the youth but was on a scale unprecedented in

Sri Lanka's modern history. It 'shook not only our complacency but our conscience'[9] and has been the most traumatic single event in recent years to have spurred creative writers in English and helped them to break through their sense of alienation, to identify themselves with mass or public concerns. In additiod to the poets, it stimulated the novelists—Ediriwira Sarachchandra to write *Curfew and a Full Moon*, James Goonewardene *Acid Bomb Explosion*, Punyakante Wijenaike *The Rebel*, M. Chandrasoma *Out Out Brief Candle* and Raja Proctor *Waiting for Surabiel*. Sarachchandra, Goonewardene and Wijenaike concentrate on the insurgency whereas Chandrasoma and Proctor traverse several decades and conclude with the insurgency.

Ashley Halpé in 'April, 1971', confronts the insurgency and acknowledges the unbridgeable gulf between the young rebels and himself :

I do not know
the thin reek of blood, the stench
of seared flesh, the
cracked irreducible bone ; I know
anly the thinner reek of pity,
the harsh edge of self-contempt,
to ashy guilt of being too old,
salaried, safe, and comfortable.

The novelists have tried to understand the insurgency in depth, and Sarachchandra, in particular, has the advantage of being steeped in Sinhala culture in which the rank and file of the rebels were rooted. He points up the crisis in society and portrays insurrectionary activity as essentially a movement of the youth of the country, youth frustrated with no hope of employment and with no faith in the existing order. He shows the youth as both callow and genuinely idealistic. When the insurgency breaks out, he shows it as ill-planned but well-intentioned. Sarachchandra is equally critical of the State as it combats the revolutionaries. The army and police are shown as crass and brutal, while the Prime Minister appears right and humane when she offers an amnesty to the rebels if they surrender and promises a fair trial. Thus Sarachchandra's view of the insurgency appears impartial and sensible. He has more sympathy for the insurgents than James Goonewardene in *Acid Bomb Explosion*, which was serialised in the *Tribune* in 1978. All Sarachchandra's rebels appear human beings, whereas Goonewardene's most prominent insurgent, Hemapala, appears a caricature.

But the main strength of Sarachchandra's novel lies in his rendering of the response of his chief character, Professor Amaradasa, to the events taking place around him and portraying the moral crises of a liberal intellectual. Professor Amaradasa, well versed in his subject, archaeology and ancient history, is a dedicated scholar, concerned about the welfare of his students, but he is out of touch with the world around him and he is teaching was irrelevant to his students' lives and needs. He typifies the reaction of many who did not take insurrectionary activity seriously till the explosion came. He had subscribed to the newspaper of the insurgent party out of impulse, not because he shared their views, and, when the rebellion breaks out, he becomes a suspect figure to the Vice Chancellor and the Police. His position becomes more complicated when, still a liberal, he cannot help but provide refuge in his home for a night to two of his students who are insurgents. Another of his students, suspected of being an insurgent, is imprisoned in the town near the University and yearns for a visit from him. The Professor is reduced to lying and evasion and suffers alone, not confiding in his affectionate and sensible wife. As the insurrection peters out, the novel moves to its climax. The Professor is required for questioning by the Police. It turns out that his wife had come to know of his subscription and advises complete denial. The novel ends on an interesting, ambiguous note. Will the Professor follow the advice of his wife and recant or will he remain true to his liberal self ?

Curfew and a Full Moon is a closely integrated, intelligent novel, one of our best works of fiction, but it is tied to the confines of a small university and the limited concerns of a university don. Raja Proctor's *Waiting for Surabiel* is more out-going and wider in scope though less finely unified. Proctor takes as his epigraph Woodrow Wilson's statement that 'the history of a nation is the history of its villages written large' and, in keeping with it, dramatizes Sri Lanka history in the making through several phases of changing rural life and the life story of his hero, a villager, Surabiel.

After providing a glimpse of the closing years of British rule in Sri Lanka, Proctor presents the period around the granting of Independence in 1948. The first General Election according to to him was a contest between the Brown Flag Party (the Rightists) and the Red Flag Party (the Leftists), both of whom claim credit for winning Independence. The watchword of the former is Slowly, slowly ! Together to the stars', while the latter favours redical and immediate changes. The Brown Flag Party wins and Proctor then introduces the next important complication in Sri Lankan Politics, the advent of the Pink Flag Party, a socialist 'Centre' Party ; styling itself the People's Party and having mass appeal, it swept the next polls. The Pink Flag Party to some extent alters the institutional structures of the country, but all the political parties succumb to a heritage of shocking corruption. Proctor calls in question the whole parliamentary system. The educated youth bring about a revolt and fail, but Proctor suggests that conditions could very well be heading for another insurrection.

Proctor telescopes history and even takes liberties—legitimate—with it. His portrayal of politics is candid and rings essentially true, and he draws sensible conclusions, while his representational, almost factual, impressions of history are convincing. The chief flaws of the novel are that Surabiel's development from villager to rebel is not convincingly negotiated and that Proctor does not contribute anything significant by way of original interpretation in his presentation of politics, and these limit his achievement to having written a good novel by local standards but not quite achieving the level of a V.S. Naipaul or Paul Scott.

Commenting on 'the complex faith of Sri Lankan creative writer who works in English,' Ashley Halpé wrote : 'there is no sustained exploration of the world these writers ought to know best—the world of the English-educated, English-speaking class—from the inside : this class has yet to produce a literature which successfully contemplates its own most profound experiences.'[10] This is precisely what James Goonewardene does in *The Awakening of Doctor Kirthi*, the title story of his recent collection of stories. Its hero is Dr. Kirthi, an exceptionally skilful surgeon, who presumably lives and works in Colombo. He is conscious of shortcomings in government hospitals, but is not discouraged : he is understanding, patriotic, even idealistic. But as time passes, Dr Kirthi, has to face more and more shortcomings without visible signs of improvement, yet he does not surrender to the tide. As he fights alone, he is brought up against ills in various sections of society : corruption amongst politicians, spinelessness among professional classes, the servility of the bureaucracy, the absence of conscientiousness in the working class. Educational policies too are criticised and, when his son becomes a victim of these, this is the last straw as far as the Doctor is concerned and he decides to emigrate. The significance of the tale, despite its flaws, transcends a concern with 'the drain brain' to encompass the larger problems of an intellectual who strives to maintain his ideals in the face of uncongenial, even hostile, conditions.

'All art is a collaboration,'[11] said J. M. Synge, and drama is particularly so. There has never been, in Sri Lanka, a relationship between playwright, stage conditions and audience, conductive to the creation of much drama in English. The audience is small, favours foreign plays, mainly Western comedies or musicals ; there is no State patronage unlike in the case of drama in the vernacular languages, and no professionalism. There is an English-language theatre but little original drama in English by Sri Lankans. One can discern three strands in the meagre body of work in this field. The historical plays include Lucien de Zoysa's efforts, the best among them, *Fortress in th Sky*, being published in 1982. It is play on the life of Kasyapa (5th centry A.D.) but while the recreation of the past in stilted, De Zoysa invests his main characters with a psychological depth which has a human relevance even today : Prince Kasyapa appears a Hamlet-like hero who is compelled to involve himself in politics and deteriorates from an idealistic individualist to an inhuman tyrant, driven by delusions of divinity. The plays of light entertainment include the hardy perennials like E.F.C. Ludowyk's farce *He Comes from Jaffna* and H.C.N. Lanerolle and E.M.W. Joseph's *Well, Mudaliyar*, a masochistic kind of play during which Sri Lankans laugh at their own use of the English language. More promising are the more recent avant-grade plays such as those of Ernest MacIntyre and Nedra Vittachi. Actually, MacIntyre is our only dramatist of any stature and any discussion of Sri Lankan drama in English would end up very much a discussion of his work. He conceives his prieces in terms of the theatre and suits his plays to the taste of the local audience by employing comedy as his vehicle to convey serious themes. Among his plays only *Loneliness of the Short-Distance Traveller* (1971) and *A Somewhat Mad and Grotesque Comedy* (1973) have been published (in the journal *New Ceylon Writing*), both showing a mastery of Absurd Drama, especially the latter, more universal in its scope, which sees violence as something eternal and provides an insight into family structures and priorities in life.

From the vantage point of 1984, Sri Lankan literature in English, especially the poetry and fiction, seems to me to have passed beyond the stage of promise, surmounted the problems of alienation, and is now being published by reputed houses abroad It too participates now in what Patrick Fernando called 'the organized internationalization of English as a creative medium.'[12]

NOTES

1. Ariya Abeysinghe & Iranganie Abeysinghe, 'Some Thoughts on the Contemporary Ceylonese Literature in English' : *New Ceylon Writing*, 1970, p. 4.
2. Lakdasa Wikkramasinha, 'Note' : *Lustre : Poems* (Kandy : Ariya, 1965), p. 51.
3. Ashley Halpé, 'Creative Writing in English' : K.M. de Silva (ed.), *Sri Lanka : A Survey* (London : Hurst, 1977), p. 452.
4. In a radio review of the book.
5. Raymond Williams, *The Country and the City* (London : Paladin, 1975), p. 9.
6. James Goonewardene, *A Quiet Place* (Colombo : K.V.G. de Silva, 1965), p. 38.

7. Punyakante Wijenaike, 'The Harvest' : *The Third Woman* (Colombo : Privately pbld, 1963), p. 3.
8. Wijenaike, 'The Promise' : *The Third Woman*, p. 112.
9. Lakshmi de Silva, 'New Poetry : Six Recent Collections' : *New Ceylon Writing*, 1973, p. 69.
10. Ashley Halpé, Editorial : *Navasilu*, I, 1976, pp. 2-3.
11. J.M. Synge, 'Preface' : *The Playboy of the Western World and other plays* (London : The New English Library, 1961), p. 7.
12. 'Yasmine Gooneratne interviews Patrick Fernando' : *Journal of South Asian Literature*, XII, 1 & 2, 1976, p. 106.

CHAPTER 5

English for University Admission

In his remarkably sensible essay "Literary Research : Thoughts for an Agenda", George Watson rightly said : "Now that English is the lingua franca of mankind, we need to study connections between learning English as a second language and studying its literature on the other . . . how the study of English poetry or literary prose can be introduced into the study of English as a second language : at what stage in that study, in what aspects, and with what results."[1] I wish to advance inquiries in this field by examining Sri Lankan experience at the stage of university admission.

In the first place, we have to find out the meaning of the phrase, "English as a second language", as applied to Sri Lanka during specific historical phases. The phrase is usually glibly employed as though its meaning were self-evident but it is really deceptive. Its meaning could change from society to society, from period to period. Japan is culturally autonomous to a high degree and the Japanese study English as a second language for such purposes as fostering commerce with English-speaking countries and acquiring scientific knowledge. The Germans and the Russians do not need English to gain any but extremely specialised knowledge and learn it to come into contact with a foreign culture. On the other hand, in such countries as Indonesia and Thailand, English is indispensable for higher education. Yet in these countries, unlike in Sri Lanka, English is for everyone a foreign language. From 1948, the year of independence, till 1956, English was the official language of Sri Lanka. It was the language of administration and of business, the language of education in the good urban schools and the language of higher education. A pass in English was compulsory if a candidate was to be awarded the Senior School Certificate, the equivalent of the General Certificate of Education (Ordinary Level). For the small but very influential minority that enjoyed the benefits of English education, English was not a "second" language, in the full sense. It was not their mother tongue, it was true, but it was the language, the used is most spheres of life, while the vernacular was the language of the kitchen and bedroom. English was one of the two half languages they used in the ordinary business of life.

In this context, the demands made on those offering English as a subject for university admission were stringent. These demands are set out in Dr. (later Professor) H.A. Passé's article, 'Education and the English Syllabus for University Entrance and H.S.C.', published in 1947, and apply during the next two decades or so. The English syllabus consisted of two papers.

> Paper I is intended to initiate the young student in general way into the tradition of English literature through the close and intensive study of specified texts. The texts have to be carefully selected; they must be of undoubted literary merit, suitable to the age group 16 to 18, and must provide a good introduction to English literature. They have to be both representative and worth while, and as only a small number of books can be selected, these must be as adequate to the purpose of the paper as possible. These purposes include a training (i) of reading capacity, and (ii) in methods of literary study.[2]

The demands of Paper I do not end here. "Historical scholarship" is needed :

> The History of English Literature is not prescribed; this does not mean that no knowledge of the history of English literature will be necessary, indeed something more than this will be needed, but this knowledge will be ancillary to the study of the texts. The student will learn something of the life and thought, the social and political history of which these works are a part; he should have some insight into the way of life and feeling this literature represents. Historical scholarship, even at this stage, is indispensable but it is instrumental, not an end itself. . . . In studying these texts the student, therefore, learns two things simultaneously; how to evaluate a work of literary art, and how to take the historical context into consideration is doing this.[3]

The student needs even more by way of equipment :

> Critical theory, like historical scholarship and linguistic studies, is an essential part of the student's equipment, but it is instrumental : all these are aids. It is the assessment of poetry that is called 'practical criticism,' but the question 'is this a good poem ?' is related to the question 'what is Poetry ?'[4]

Thus, the student is expected to be a complete critic at his level. The criteria for the selection of texts, purposes of the paper and its demands on the student are the same as those for students whose mother tongue is English. The type of question set at the examination is in keeping with the requirements of the paper :

> The questions set on these books must be of such a kind as will give both students and teachers the right orientation. Questions of the type 'Write an appreciation of . . .' are as easy to set as to answer, they involve no knowledge in the asking, and can be answered with no first hand knowledge of the text. Questions which merely solicit facts about the texts are, of course, a gift to the crammer and the coach. The best type of question is that which itself offers a criticism and asks the candidate to confirm or refute it from the evidence of his own reading. A question such as that set at the December, 1946, examination: " 'Herbert is a sincere and sensitive poet and an accomplished artist.' Discuss" does not merely ask for facts, though it certainly demands a knowledge of the text; it requires at a certain level, a critical approach and some skill in the selection and arrangement of material.[5]

The second paper had the elastic title "General English". As the syllabus for 1948 says :

> "The paper will contain passages of prose and verse for criticism. Candidates may also be required to write an essay on a literary subject and to answer questions relating to their reading This paper is intended to test the candidate's ability to read sensitively and intelligently, whether it is a newspaper, advertisement, poem or novel he is dealing with, and to express himself efficiently. Candidates will be expected to have some knowledge of the way in which language works

and the various purposes for which it is used; to be able to distinguish between different kinds of writing and to determine the aims, methods, sensibility and skilfulness of a writer by examining the way in which he uses language."

The relation of this paper to the one on Prescribed Texts is close. It is intended partly to help the student to acquire the technique of reading needed for dealing with the prescribed texts, and beyond that it emphasizes the connexion between reading well and writing well, and the relation to these skills to general intelligence and sensibility, and the adequacy of one's response to the difficult and complex conditions of modern living.[6]

The purposes of this paper and its demands on the student are the same as those for students whose mother tongue is English. The requirements of the English syllabus (taken as a whole) for admission to the University of Sri Lanka were the same as those for admission to British universities such as London, Cambridge and Oxford ; and of course, the requirements of British universities applied to native speakers of English and their overseas students were expected to measure up to these. In a word, the syllabus was well-conceived but inappropriate.

Because of the extremely stringent requirements for admission to the English course at the University of Ceylon, those who did succeed in being admitted were students of high quality. I remember reading an article in a newspaper, *The Times of Ceylon*, by Mr. Robin Mayhead, written during his term as a Visiting Lecturer at our University in the mid-1950s (he is now Reader in English at the University of Stirling) in which he stated that the students offering English at the University of Ceylon were of such quality that any university in the world ought to be proud to have them. All Ceylonese students in English who went to Britain to read for post-graduate degrees after completing their B.A. degree at our university, have been successful. But those stringent requirements to enter the English course at our university, had their deleterious aspects, especially in the long run. English was reputed to be a difficult subject and its reputation was justified. Students were discouraged from offering the subject and only a few were both brave and good enough to select it as one of their subjects, still fewer passed in it. Thus, those who were trained in English at the university were very few indeed—approximately twenty each year. Out of this twenty, only a handful entered the teaching profession and thus the spread of English was impeded. The dearth of teachers of English today, which has reached the proportions of a crisis, can be traced to those stringent requirements for university admission during the decades soon after independence. The university shut out students of a quality which has been regarded as good enough in the 1970s. Those stringent requirements seemed proper to the powerful English-educated elite and were accepted by them unquestioningly probably because these ensured the continuation of their privileged position. The university authorities, in fact, modelled our syllabuses on those of British universities and were anxious to maintain British standards. They do not seem to have realised the implications of the key fact that English was not our mother tongue and the implications of the fact that our social needs were going to be different from Britain's. They themselves were members of the English-educated elite and were not responsive to the needs of other sections of our society. In effect, they sacrificed the larger interests of the country as a whole. Their blindness is a consequence of our colonial past, of British-oriented thinking and is, I suspect, common to many excolonies of Britain. It is more difficult to break intellectual shackles than political fetters because these are more insidious. Intellectual independence comes after, usually long after political independence. Thus, I do not wish to berate the English Department of the University or adopt an attitude of superiority. It is much easier today to be critical of colonial influence and think independently.

The year 1956 is, in many ways, a watershed in recent Ceylon history. English was dethroned from its position as the official language of Sri Lanka. Sinhala was installed in its place and became the language of administration, while both Sinhala and Tamil became language of education and gradually began to displace English. The common man began to matter and the influence of the English-educated elite began to decrease little by little. But the English Department at the University was not responsive to the winds of change and the requirements for university admission remained the same for virtually another decade. In the late 1960s it was obvious that the standard of English in the schools had deteriorated as a cosequence of the primary stress on the vernacular. It was right that English should be the second language of students but it was unduly neglected. A pass in English was no longer compulsory for a student to obtain the G.C.E. (Ordinary Level) and the psychology of students is such that they neglected subjects which are not strictly necessary for success at examinations. It looks as though the English Department made its syllabus, in particular Paper II, simpler because it needed students to survive rather than because it had pondered the new role of English in Sri Lanka. Still, the syllabus on the whole aimed at fairly high standard partly because the Department thought this was necessary to ensure the high level of competence which employers and 'society' expected from graduates in English. This is the kind of syllabus in force today for the General Certificate of Education (Advanced Level).

The syllabus of Paper I of the G.C.E. (Advanced Level), at first glance, looks like its earlier equivalent but is, in several ways, a departure from it. The current texts are Shakespeare's *Othello,* Ibsen's *An Enemy of the people*, Arthur Miller's *Death of a Salesman*, E.M. Forster's *A Passage to India.* Leonard Woolf's *The Village in the Jungle*, an anthology of *Twentieth Century Short Stories* (it consists of Joseph Conrad's *The Secret Sharer*, D.H. Lawrence's *Odour of Chrysanthemums*, Saki's *The Lumber Room*, E.M. Forster's *The Machine Stops* and Garham Greene's *The Destructors*) and *Selections of English Poetry* (it consists of four groups of poems : Group I—Shakespeare's 'Shall I compare thee to a summer's day ?' 'Full many a glorious morning . . . ' 'My Mistress' eyes . . .'; Thomas Campion's 'Cherry-Ripe' and 'Laura'; John Donne's 'Song', 'The Good Morrow', 'Sweetest Love......', 'Death, be not proud' ; Group II– William Wordsworth's 'I wandered lonely as a cloud', 'Three years she grew in sun and shower', 'Earth has not anything to show more fair' ; John Keats' 'On first looking into Chapman's Homer', 'Ode to Autumn', 'La Belle Dame Sans Merci' ; Group III—W.B. Yeats' 'A Prayer for my Daughter', T.S. Eliots' 'Journey of the Magi', Edmund Blunden's 'A Hong Kong House', D. H. Lawrence's 'Baby Tortoise'; Group

IV—Zulfikar Ghose's 'This Landscape; These People', Dom Moraes' 'Autobiography', Gabriel Okara's 'Piano and Drums,' David Rubadiri's 'Stanley Meets Mutesa'). The syllabus prescribes mainly modern literature. Most of the texts are from the period after 1880; Ibsen's play Arthur Miller's play, E.M Forster's novel. Leonard Woolf's novel, the short stories and two out of the four groups of poems are modern literature. The student would, certainly, acquire a sense of the variety of modern writing. Whereas the earlier syllabus intended to initiate the student into "the tradition of English literature", this syllabus tries to introduce students to several traditions and, within the limits of a syllabus for university admission, it can prescribe only one long text or a few short poems to represent each tradition. Ibsen's play represents European traditions, while Arthur Miller's play represents the entire American tradition. Leonard Woolf's novel represents literature about Sri Lanka. When we come to the area of Commonwealth Literature, we find that Indian literature in English is represented by two short poems, one each by Zulfikar Ghose and Dom Moraes, while African literature in English is represented by two poems, one each by Gabriel Okara and David Rubadiri : there is nothing, say, from Australian, Canadian or Caribbean literature. The syllabus-makers are not averse to selecting per-modern literature and this vast, rich field is represented only by a Shakespeare play and two small groups of poems. I think the syllabus is trying to represent too many areas and also areas which are too vast and too diverse; as a consequence, each area is barely touched and the syllabus appears something of a hotchpotch. The criterion of "undoubted literary merit", which seems to me valuable, has, in effect and probably unconsciously, been modified and even discarded in some instances. Ibsen's *An Enemy of the People* is a weak play. One of the aims of the *Selections of English Poetry* is 'to stimulate students into making of comparative evaluations'[7] and this has led to the inclusion of many feeble poems; the prescribed sonnets of Shakespeare are among his weaker efforts in this genre; the two lyrics by Campion are undistinguished; Donne's 'Song', 'Go and Catch a falling star' is one of his immature poems, while David Rubadiri's 'Stanley Meets Mutesa' is a superficial poem. It is obvious that the texts should be "suitable to the age group 16 to 18", yet this principal has not been consistently applied. As Dr. H. A. Passé says, "It is important to select texts to which, *at this level*, a worthwhile response is likely. *This is not the same thing as selecting texts 'within the experience' of this age group; indeed few books would be within the experience of young people of this age, the books themselves assist is deepening and widening experience.*"[8] From this point of view, *Othello* is too complex and difficult. *Romeo and Juliet* or *Julius Caesar*, which have been prescribed in earlier years, are far more suitable. Young students are likely to respond to the social comedy of *A passage to India* but are certain to baffled by its metaphysical side. They would find Donne's poems too difficult and the last three lines of 'The Good Morrow', in particular, would be absolutely impenetrable. Arthur Miller's *Death of a Salesman* is too intimately related to the American way of life with its myth of success and popularity and non-sufficiently relevant to our lives in Sri Lanka today.

The questions set on this syllabus are at different levels. For instance, the 1977 question paper contained questions of the same general standard as the 1950s :

> "It is the meaning which the jungle assumes in Mr. Woolf's novel which lifts it above the level of a romantic novel in an exotic Eastern setting." Discuss.

It contained a question which was as difficult as any in the preceding years and which relates to critical theory :

> "All good poetry is this spontaneous overflow of powerful feeling . . . " (Wordsworth). Attempt a critical evaluation of this view of poetry, supporting your answer by analysing examples taken from poems you have studied.

It also contains questions simpler than those of the 1950s :

> Choosing any two scenes from *Death of a Salesman* in which flashbacks are used, show whether the flashbacks are related to the situation in the present.

It could be argued that questions at different levels cater to students of differing capabilities. But I am inclined to think that difficult questions should not be set. Difficult questions would be avoided by the average student, discourage him and reduce his choice of questions. The student of more-than-average ability who dares to answer difficult questions may score less than if he were to answer simple questions or score less than candidates answering simple questions. I advocate simple questions and a uniform level for the questions.

Paper II of the G.C.E. (Advanced Level) is simpler than the kind of paper set earlier. The earlier question paper consisted entirely of questions in the "practical criticism" of unseen passages of prose and verse. Today the paper begins with an essay question; students are asked to write an essay on a current general topic (for instance, the topics in the 1977 question paper include 'The 1976 Non-aligned Conference held in Sri Lanka', 'Tourism in Sri Lanka' and 'The Convertible Rupee Account System in Sri Lanka'). This is followed by a precis question. The students are asked for the meanings of individual words and asked to correct faulty sentences; questions of this sort would have been unthinkable in the 1950s because they would have been considered far too elementary. There is a prose passage with questions on it, questions not as difficult as normal "practical criticism". There is one "practical criticism" question, at the end of the question paper, only one such question and that question is optional.

The whole syllabus, which was an uneasy compromise between principles of syllabus-making and the bread-and-butter need of students for the Department of English, without any pondering of fundamentals, did enable the Department to limp along The Department now admits students it would have shut out in the 1950s and still the numbers have dwindled, though not to the point of extinction. The number of teachers of English recruited from graduates has decreased to less than a handful, while the demand for teachers has increased with the need to provide students in schools all over the island (not just the fortunate few as in the past) with facilities for the study of English. To tide over the crisis, the Ministry of Education recruited as teachers those with G.C.E. (Advanced Level) and even those with G.C.E. (Ordinary Level) qualifications in English. This solution was far from satisfactory. The paper in English language at the G.C.E. (O.L.) for the last ten years has been set at such a low level that candidates can pass it without being able to speak or write connected English. One can imagine the damage those ill-qualified teachers inflict on their pupils. Speakers of English have increased considerably over the years. The report of the Census of Ceylon for 1946 gives the following information in respect of the population three years of age and over who are able to speak a language :

Total population able to speak a language :	6,158,187	
Ability to speak English only :	11,703	0.2%
Ability to speak both English and Sinhalese	178,224	2.9%
Ability to speak both English and Tamil :	63,104	1.0%
Ability to speak English, Sinhalese and Tamil :	149,245	2.4%[9]

The Report of the Census of Ceylon for 1953 gives 648,331 as the English literate population 5 years of age and over.[10] In 1946, the total population was 6,657,339, while in 1953 it was 8,097,895. The rate of literacy in English has increased much faster than the rate of population. Speakers of English are now more widely scattered about the island than earlier and they generally speak an English of poorer quality that the English-educated elite of old. Thus, the pressures for more and better education in English are extremely intense and the need for qualified teachers of English poses very acute problems.

From 1948 till the 1970s, the syllabus in English for university admission was not properly adjusted to local conditions and the role of English as a second language in these conditions. The first serious attempt at adjustment came in the mid-1970s when a syllabus for the Higher National Certificate of Education (HNCE, for short), was formulated. The HNCE was to replace the G.C E. (Advanced Level) and it was a part of the many reforms introduced by the Ministry of Education of the time. The HNCE syllabus Committee for English thought :

> . . . the content of the English literature syllabus at A-Level (which the HNCE will now replace) has not changed substantially since the days of the University Entrance Examination 35 years ago. This in spite of the vast changes in the social

context of the teaching of English in Sri Lanka over these years.

> The A-level syllabus still consists of a group of prescribed texts chosen to illustrate the history of English literature from Shakespeare to the twentieth century. The few occasional and minor deviations into American literature (selections from Frost have been sometimes prescribed) or more recently into Commonwealth poetry (of which there are a few examples in the current A-Level anthology) don't alter the general character of the syllabus.[11]

The HNCE Committee was right in seeing a need to reform the existing syllabus and in trying to diagnose the past. But the Committee did not see that several criteria were used in selecting texts in the past and that there is a marked difference between the A-Level syllabus today and the earlier syllabus for the University Entrance Examination. So the diagnosis is sweeping and ill-informed.

The remedies of the HNCE Committee were embodied in an anthology, *Reading with Understanding*, which the Committee compiled :

> This single anthology, which includes extracts of both prose and verse, replaces the set books from English literature of the old syllabus. But the purpose of this change is not merely to substitute one book for many. This anthology is intended to serve as the focus of a new approach to the teaching of English at this level.[12]

This anthology was compiled on the basis of several principles, which the Committee thought were new, even revolutionary :

> In our choice of extracts, we have adopted the principle that the anthology should be directed towards teaching not English literature but literature through the medium of the English language. Accordingly, the extracts have been taken from a variety of sources, including translations from other literatures into English.

The "variety of sources" is great. Let us first note the writers writing originally in English. The British writers include Blake, Dickens,

Hardy, D.H. Lawrence, Orwell, A.P. Herbert, Leonard Woolf, Roger McGough and the Beatles. The American writers include Hemingway ; the humorists James Thurber, Ogden Nash, Frank Sullivan and Don Marquis ; the sociologist Eric Fromm ; Black American writers such as Eldridge Cleaver. William J. Harris and James Weldon Johnson. There is a poem by the African writer Wole Soyinka ; a poem by the Indian writer, Nissim Ezekiel ; and an essay by Satyajith Ray, India's greatest film-maker. There are also poems by Sri Lankans, Yasmine Gooneratne and Anne Ranasinghe. Secondly, let us note the translated writers. These include the Italian Ignazio Silone, the Frenchman Jacques Prevert, the Spaniards Federico Garcia Lorca and Antonio Machado, the Chilean Pablo Neruda. There are several mediaeval Chinese poems translated by Arthur Waley and Ezra Pound. There is a poem by Mahadeviyakka, an Indian woman poet of the 12th century who wrote in the Kannada language, and a short story by the modern Hindi writer, Premchand.

The HNCE Committee explained why it prescribed "not English literature but literature through the medium of the English language" :

> English literature can no longer have for us the special privileged status, as compared with other foreign literatures, that it possessed under colonial rule and in the penumbra of a colonial culture even after independence. On the other hand, we have to recognize that English remains, and will remain in the immediately foreseeable future, the main medium of access to international literature (which includes of course, the best English literature itself). In spite of the increasing number of persons learning foreign languages other than English (a welcome development), it is likely that for a long time to come many readers and translators will approach the great works of literature in other languages through the medium of English versions.
>
> For us today, therefore, the literary importance of English is that it is a gateway not only to Shakespeare, Blake or Dickens, but also to Li Po, Stendhal, Tolstoy or Brecht.
>
> With this new function of English in mind, one of the

first decisions the HNCE Committee took was to abandon the traditional prescribed texts from English literature.

It really has *long* been a function of English to be, for us, the gateway not only to English literature but to other foreign literatures as well. Moreover, there is nothing new in the realisations of this "function". The University Entrance Examination and the A-Level syllabuses have included literature in English translation such as Chekov's *The Cherry Orchard* and Ibsen's *An Enemy of the People*, while if we look at English syllabuses at the university, it turns out that these have included Stendhal, Tolstoy, Brecht and other non-British writers in English, translations. But hitherto syllabuses in English, particularly at the level of university admission, have prescribed mainly English literature. I accept, as a general principle, that English literature should not occupy a colonial kind of position, yet to prescribe now mainly English literature for students of English is logical and not necessarily a consequence of colonial thinking. Indeed, it is colonial thinking to notice a tendency in England towards the teaching of literature in English rather than English literature, to come under its influence and regard it as "more pertinent" to us, as a prominent member of the HNCE Committee argued.[13] Unless there is a radical change in the whole existing framework of syllabuses, non-English literatures, if they are to be of *central* significance, belong to their own respective courses of study—Stendhal to French, Tolstoy to Russian, Brecht to German and so on. Students gain by being initiated into a whole valuable tradition and, from a practical point of view, it is not possible to initiate students at the level of university admission into more than one tradition. Moreover all syllabuses in English from the University Entrance Examination to the H.N.C.E. want to train young students to be sensitive to words, and students do not quite get this training when they are reading translations. They respond directly not to the original words of writers but to the words of translators. Oscar Wilde wrote of women : "it is better to be beautiful than to be good. But . . . it is better to be good than to be ugly."[14]

Translators have the same kind of aims and a translation cannot be an exact reproduction of the original. If translations are to be prescribed for study, they should be selected with greater care than original works : the translation of Mahadeviyakka's metaphysical poem, 'Like a Silk Worm Weaving', is unimpressive, whatever the merits of the original. The H.N.C.E. Anthology, then, has far too much translated metter for students at the beginning of their literary training. The extracts are rooted in such a diversity of cultures and written in such a diversity of styles that tend to bewilder the young student. In fact, it would not be too much of an exaggeration to say that the HNCE Anthology seems to be trying to introduce the student to the literature of the whole world in the course of one short book. The syllabus for University admission should be linked with the syllabus at the university and form an introduction to it. One of my objections to the translations from Chinese and Japanese is that these are not covered by this important consideration.

The extracts in the HNCE Anthology "have been arranged in relation to eleven themes. These represent the aspects of experience that we believe to be of interest and importance to the adolescent growing up in Sri Lanka today."[15] The HNCE Committee, in fact, has merely rephrased the earlier criterion that the literature prescribed should be suitable to the age group of the students. Though the criterion is not new as the H.N.C.E. Committee claimed,[16] it is sound. The selected themes are Family, Love, School and Learning Society, War, Our Natural World. The Arts and Creativity, The World of Work, Leisure, Identity and the World of Ideas. There is also a section entitled Drama. The themes seem to embrace virtually the whole of life! As a consequence. none of the themes are presented substantially and well so that students could get their teeth into them as it were. For instance, let us consider the five pieces under the heading, 'Family'. The short extract from D.H. Lawrence's *Sons and Lovers* and Jacques Prevert's short translated poem 'Breakfast' reveal aspects of estrangement, yet, together, they do not constitute a meaty presentation of this facet of life. Nissim Ezekiel's short poem 'Night of the Scorpion'. D.H. Lawrence's even shorter poem 'Piano'. and Ignazio Silone's translated very short story, 'Return to Fontamara' embody aspects of family life which are diverse and only flimsily interconnected. Similarly, under the heading 'Society'. Wole Soyinka's poem 'Telephone Conversation' is included, yet it is the only item on the subject of racial discrimination. Other references to this subject in extracts chosen to illustrate other themes (for instance, Eldridge Cleaver's essay 'The Muhammed Ali – Patterson Fight' in the section on 'Leisure') do not add upto much. Drama is seriously neglected. There is only one play, an extremely short one, and that a translation of a Japanese Kyogen play. 'The Bird-Catcher in Hell'. Teachers have complained that young students find it difficult to get to grips with many of the extracts. They find Eldridge Cleaver's essay difficult to understand. They find it difficult to grasp that Thurber's 'The Secret Life of Walter Mitty' is not just funny, but pathetic as well.

The H.N.C.E. syllabus raises other issues of interest :

> The anthology is intended to present to the student various kinds of writing: informative, argumentative, descriptive, emotional, imaginative and creative. We have not restricted our conception of literature to creative writing alone, though this has been given its due representation in this anthology. We hope that through the reading of these extracts the student will obtain an understanding of the various ways in which language is used as a means of expression and communication.

I am very much in favour of the syllabus for university admission covering literature in this broad sense. An exclusive diet of creative writing has been known to set up barriers against the appreciation of other kinds of writing. We need to know areas of thought in non-creative prose if we are to be reasonably alive to our age. Most students would not continue their studies beyond the HNCE stage; their future lives will demand that they read and write non-creative prose. This applies to those who enter the university too, they will, after obtaining their degrees, usually enter the ranks of administrative service, the teaching profession or the mercantile sector.

I favour another decision of the HNCE Committee:

> Under the new scheme decided on by the Education Ministry authorities, English literature will not be a subject for the NCGE (the National Certificate of General Education, which is the equivalent of the GCE Ordinary Level), so that the first occasion when students will be studying literature in English will be when they come up to the HNCE class. Mindful of this fact, as well as of the linguistic problems of students

> for whom English is strictly a foreign language today, the HNCE Committee decided to confine its selections to prose and verse written in the idiom of modern English Inevitably, therefore, the emphasis has been mainly on contempory writing.[17]

The HNCE Committee added:

> We hope that students will find this anthology easier, in a sense, to read than the former set books because the material in it will be linguistically more within their reach than a play of Shakespeare or a poem of Donne.[18]

The assumption that earlier literature is necessarily more difficult than modern literature is false, but it is sound to prescribe for study simple modern literature in modern idiom. I would emphasize that the literature prescribed should be simple because the HNCE Anthology itself contains material which is too difficult for our young students and the Anthology does not set up a proper standard. The omission of Shakespeare from the HNCE syllabus led to much controversy. In fact, Shakespeare is not compulsory even for the G.C.E. (Advanced Level). While it is presumptuous for any of us to claim to understand all there is to any play of Shakespeare, it is true young students in Sri Lanka today find a major play of Shakespeare like *Othello* beyond them, from the point of view of its language and the experience it offers. Should one then prescribe a play like *Romeo and Juliet*? Theoretically speaking, the experience it offers ought to be appreciated by young students but our students would find its Elizabethan English too difficult a barrier to surmount. Moreover *Romeo and Juliet* though famous, is not a major work of art. One could select modern literature comparable in intensity to Shakespeare's less demanding plays (for instance, a tale by D.H. Lawrence) and this literature would have the immense advantage of being written in modern idiom. On the other hand, Professor Ashley Halpé had a point when he said :

> What is one to say of a syllabus that allows near-adult school-leavers of seventeen or eighteen to complete their course in total ignorance of the major experience in their chosen field?[19]

It is, certainly, a matter for great regret that generally speaking, young students cannot respond to Shakespeare, but the fact has to be faced. Yet it should be open to any student to read Shakespeare if he can or if he can be trained to do so. I guess there will be exceptions to the general rule: after all, many a student answers the questions on Shakespeare at the G.C.E. (A Level) Examination. It was reassuring when Mr. Reggie Siriwardene, voicing the view of the HNCE Committee, said :

> As for Shakespeare, if any student is capable of reading him and wants to read him, nobody has put him on the Index.[20]

The HNCE Anthology contained extracts from an unusual variety of sources, yet it had a central organising principle :

> We intend that every extract, whether a translation of an ancient Chinese poem or a piece of contemporary journalism, should be read for its relevance to human experience today.[21]

The principle is sound, but the HNCE Committee made an undue fuss about it in the columns of our newspapers. It is a truism that good literature is universal in its appeal. If texts of "undoubted literary merit"(to see Dr. Passé's formulation in 1947) were chosen, these would be relevant to human experience today. Similarly, the HNCE Committee thought:

> The most important aim of the anthology can be summed up in the concluding sentence of the introduction: "Our purpose has been not to make the study of literature a self-sufficient end in itself but to use it as a means of broadening the students' awareness and their comprehension of contemporary life and society".[22]

The aim is sound, but not new. In Similar terms, in 1947, Dr. Passé referred to "the connexion between reading and writing well, and the relation of these skills to the adequacy of one's response to the difficult and complex conditions of modern living".[23] The 'Introduction' to *Selections of English Poetry for the G.C.E. Advanced Level Examination* concluded :

> . . . The study of literature gives us the opportunity, therefore, to feel life in greater variety than we can reach by

> ourselves, and to feel it with greater intensity and depth of understanding. We talk so much about improving our standard of living; it is vital to remember that poetry can improve the quality of our living.[24]

The HNCE Committee proudly wrote :

> But, in another sense, this anthology will be a more exacting test of their capacity to read intelligently and sensitively (than the former set of books). It will not be possible, we hope, to prepare students for the examination paper on this anthology by dictating to them notes drawn from a history of literature or from critical works. Both teachers and students will be obliged to confront the text itself and make their own responses to it.[25]

This aim, in its essence, is sound but not new. Earlier syllabus-makers too wanted students and teachers to make their own responses to the prescribed texts. Dr. Passé wrote in 1947: "These texts are to be regarded not as so much subject-matter to be memorised, but as material for training young people to read intelligently and sensitively, to make first-hand contacts with good writers, and to learn what literary art is, how it works and what it does for us".[26] The G.C.E. Advanced Level syllabus-maker wanted "to stimulate students into close and sensitive reading."[27] But the HNCE is over ambitious The earlier texts were such that teachers and students sought, and received, help from histories of literature and critical works, yet, I think the HNCE Committee is mistaken in depriving them of this kind of help. I think that our teachers and students are such that they need this help and this is not something to be ashamed of, in our context. The exercises that follow each extract in the HNCE Anthology, amount to more or less "Practical Criticism", the familiar method of approaching literature since the 1940s in Sri Lanka. The HNCE Committee said:

> In the exercises we have tried to steer clear of technical critical jargon, the bane of literary studies (as far as we are aware, the word symbol doesn't occur anywhere in the questions).[28]

Earlier syllabus-makers too wanted students to avoid jargon. It is no sin to use the word, symbol, if it is the most appropriate word in a given context.

The HNCE syllabus was introduced in 1971. The Government changed in 1977 and the new Ministry of Education decided to revert to the G C.E. Advanced Level There has been no HNCE examination and it is therefore not possible to discuss the level of its questions. Yet I would guess that its question papers would be as demanding as its equivalents at the G C.E. Advanced Level. The HNCE Committee was right in thinking that the English syllabus needed to be reformed, but its remedies have a mixed value. Some of its proposals were not as original as it thought they were. Some of the sound proposals were, in effect merely a rephrasing of old principles. Some of its new proposals were misguided, while the others were sound.

My own positive proposals for today's English syllabus at the level of university admission have been partly indicated by my discussion of earlier syllabuses. I assume that students will be required to answer two question papers and it is logical to have one paper on literature and other on language. Let us first discuss the literature paper. The texts should be of "undoubted literary merit" and "suitable to the age group 16 to 18". I would regard an attempt "to initiate the young student into the tradition of English literature" or an attempt to illustrate the history of English literature as being outside the scope of the syllabus. The texts should be in modern idiom and written originally in English. The English used should be Standard English or good Lankan English which is an offshoot of Standard English. Our students today at the level of university admission are unsure of their English and their development would be retarded if they are introduced to other varieties of English at this stage. To limit the selection of texts in this way is not to be illiberal but to be pedagogically sound The texts should include both imaginative and non-imaginative literature. Learning could begin with easy non-imaginative prose so that students could acquire a grounding in the language. Imaginative prose should come before poetry ; though historically poetry preceded prose, our students invariably find prose easier to tackle. One of the texts could be an anthology consisting of extracts in prose and verse on a few simple themes likely to be of interest to young students It should be no more demanding than that anthology, popular in India and used in Sri Lanka too, *Modern English Prose for College Classes* edited by K.R. Chandrasekaran and K.N. Acharya Students should also learn to get to grips with longer works I would recommend for study a novel which is both simple and interesting such as Leonard Woolf's *The Village in the Jungle*. Students should also understand drama: I would recommend for study a play which is both simple and interesting such as Bernard Shaw's *Widower's Houses*. At Sri Lanka's present stage of development, it is important to extend the sympathies of, or awaken the social conscience of, our future citizens who are our present-day students; this is another reason why I should select for a syllabus novels like Woolf's or plays like Shaw's. Of course, I am completely against prescribing literature to serve a narrow propagandistic purpose. I would recommend material which is simpler than that generally prescribed by our syllabuses to date and I would not demand an ability to carry out "practical criticism". I would demand only a basic understanding of texts and a basic ability to write English. The most that should be demanded by way of critical training is the use of "the modest and familiar tool-kit of traditional grammar—parts of speech, the tense, mood and voice of verbs, problems of word-order."[29] At the examination, I would regard as typical questions these on *The Village in the Jungle*.

(1) Why was Beddegama completely overrun by the jungle ?

(2) Discuss the character of Silindu.

I would set simple questions on theme and character if I were to examine students on their prescribed texts. In respect of the second paper on language, I would recommend a simplified version of the present G.C.E. Advanced Level syllabus and at the examination, demand and ability to write an essay on a simple subject, an ability to write a simple precis, an ability to use given words in sentences so as to bring out their meaning and an ability to correct faulty sentences. I would replace the questions on "practical criticism" with questions on basic understanding of given extracts.

From one aspect, I may seem to be advocating a lowering of standards. But "lowering of standards" is not an accurate description of my approach. What I am recommending is really an appropriate syllabus, an adjustment of the English syllabus to conditions of Sri Lanka today and the role of English as a second language in these conditions. The standard of English in our schools has declined and English is strictly a foreign language to our present-day students. If we divide students into the sheep and the goats, the sheep offer science subjects while the goats offer subjects in the Humanities. The causes for this division are many students in the sciences have better prospects of employment ; the Ceylon Civil Service, which consisted of the cream of the posts in the administration and which held a considerable attraction for students in the Arts by way of prestige and remuneration, has been abolished. Yet what concerns me here is not these causes but the prospect that this division is likely to persist. There is a severe dearth of good teachers of English. The university should take the responsibility of teaching higher criticism and admit as large a number of students as possible, provided that they meet basic reuirements. The university has to provide the schools with more and better teachers of English as quickly as possible. English is, for us, the main medium of access to international knowledge and international contacts. Mr. Gunadasa Amerasekera, one of our leading Sinhalese writers and intellectuals, wrote :

> The last twenty years have shown us in very clear terms that in every field of knowledge—let it be medicine, science or the humanities—translations are completely inadequate and worthless to fill the void which has been left by the displacement of English.[30]

What we should try to do is give the mass of the people a command of English as a second language. At the moment a command of English is the preserve of a privileged minority and in these circumstances there can be no equality of opportunity. As there is a great deal of snobbery surrounding the study of English in the upper forms of the few schools that teach it as a subject for university admission and in the university, it is necessary to say that there is nothing to be ashamed of if we make simpler demands on our candidates for university admission. Warren K. Wowczuk has informed us of basic composition courses being taught to first-year university students in the United States of America and said :

> Shocking as it may seem, the average American first year university student has so little formal grasp of his language, so little certainty about using it, and such great difficulty in comprehending a page of even the most lucid modern prose that by any reasonable standard he must be regarded as a non-native speaker.[31]

If we make simpler demands on our candidates for university admission, it does not necessarily follow that our graduates will be less capable than they are at present or that the standard of our Bachelor of Arts degree will be lower than it is. An important corollary of my proposal for an appropriate syllabus in English for university admission is that the English Department should take an additional responsibility for the training of graduates *and* discharge it efficiently so that the end-product will be no less good than it is today. After all, though the university may admit students linguistically less capable than earlier, the intelligence of these students is not inferior and can be trained to reach the standard set earlier for students at the end of their course. In fact, by opening the gates wider, the university will admit students from sections of society hitherto not represented in the English Department and will draw on hitherto untapped talent If the English Department finds itself unable to maintain British standards at Final Examination for the B. A. Degree, I suggest that we discard these and set up *decent* local standards to suit local conditions and needs.

NOTES

1. George Watson, 'Literary Research; Thoughts for an Agenda': *Times Literary Supplement*, 25 February, 1977, p. 213.
2. H.A. Passé, 'Education and the English Syllabus for Univertity Entrance and H.S.C.' : *University of Ceylon Review*, Vol. 5, No. 2, October 1947, p. 6.
3. H.A. Passé, op. cit. p. 6.
4. H.A. Passé op. cit., pp. 9-10.
5. H.A. Passé, op. cit., p. 7.
6. H.A. Passé, op. cit., p. 5.

7. Ashley Halpé and D.M. de Silva, 'Introduction' : *Selections of English Poetry* (Sri Lanka: Department of Educational Publications, 1972), p. i.
8. H.A. Passé, op. cit., p. 6.
9. *Census of Ceylon 1946* (Sri Lanka : Department of Census and Statistics, 1952) Vol 4, p. 794.
10. *Census of Ceylon 1953* (Sri Lanka : Department of Census and Statistics, 1960), Vol. 3, Part 1, p. 512.
11. A.J. Gunawardene, Ranjit Gunawardene and Reggie Siriwardene, 'Teaching Literature : a new approach' : *Ceylon Daily News*, 12 June, 1976, p. 4.
12. 'A Word to the Teacher' : *Reading with Understanding* (Sri Lanka : Department of Educational Publications, 1976), p. xi.
13. Reggie Siriwardene, 'Letter to a student' : *The Sunday Times* (Sri Lanka), 24 October, 1976, p. 5.
14. Oscar Wilde, *The Picture of Dorian Gray* : G.F. Maine (ed.), *The Works of Oscar Wilde* (London and Glasgow : Collins, 1954 ed.) p. 147.
15. 'A Word to the Teacher' : *Reading with Understanding*, p. xi.
16. A.J. Gunawardene, Ranjit Gunawardene and Reggie Siriwardene, 'Teaching Literature : a new approach : *Ceylon Daily News*, 12 June, 1976, p. 4 ; Ranjit Gunawardene, H.N.C.E. Anthology, and the Critics' : *The Sunday Times* (Sri Lanka), 7 November, 1976, p. 9.
17. A.J. Gunawardene, Ranjit Gunawardene and Reggie Siriwardene, Teaching 'Literature : a new approach : *Ceylon Daily News*, 12 June, 1976, p. 4.
18. 'A Word to the Teacher' : *Reading with Understanding*, p. xii.
19. Ashley Halpé, 'Students who opt for English need a better deal' : *The Sunday Times* (Sri Lanka), 31 October, 1976, p. 5.
20. Reggie Siriwardene, 'A little bit of England' : *The Sunday Times* (Sri Lanka), 7 November, 1976, p. 5.
21. 'A Word to the Teacher' : *Reading with Understanding*, p. xi.

22. A.J. Gunawardene, Ranjit Gunawardene, and Reggie Siriwardene : 'Teaching Literature : a new approach' : *Ceylon Daily News*, 12 June, 1976, p. 4.
23 H.A. Passé, op. cit., p. 5.
24. Ashley Halpé and D.M. de Silva, 'Introduction' : *Selections of English Poetry*, p. vii.
25. 'A Word to the Teacher' : *Reading with Understanding*, p. xii.
25. H.A. Passé, op. cit., p. 6.
27 Ashley Halpé and D.M. de Silva, op. cit., p. i.
28. A.J. Gunawardene, Ranjit Gunawardene, Reggie Siriwardene, op. cit., p. 4.
29. George Watson, op. cit., p. 213.
30. Gunadasa Amerasekara, 'English and the Sinhala writer – a reply' : *The Sunday Times* (Sri Lanka), 23 January, 1977, p. 4.
31. Warren K. Wowczuk, 'Literary Research' : *Times Literary Supplement*, 6 April, 1977, p. 433.

CHAPTER 6

Forgotten Nineteenth-century Fiction: William Arnold's Oakfield and William Knighton's Forest Life in Ceylon

Slave 'operations were conducted on so great a scale that in the 20 years before the opening of the eighteenth century 300,000 slaves were exported from Africa by the English, and in the 80 years which followed, over 600,000 slaves were landed in the Island of Jamaica alone'.[1] The slaves and the convicts left behind works which appear to be artistically very poor and evoke little interest.[2] So did anti-slavery agitators like William Roscoe and James Currie.[3] But as far as I know, the British slave-traders were not spurred to writing even of this order, perhaps because of the type of men they were or because of the brutalizing nature of their occupation or both. On the other hand, from the 1830s when the Government took charge of virtually all the imperial activities of the British, it began to employ the kind of people among whom were individuals with creative or intellectual powers. It was two colonial officials, William Arnold and William Knighton, who wrote *Oakfield* (1853) and *Forest Life in Ceylon* (1854), respectively. Their works are not artistically outstanding ; but they have a value because in mid-Victorian times no Englishman thought and felt as creatively about 'undeveloped' countries in their own right as they did.

It is profitless to discuss the pedestrian language, loose organization, or moralizing stretches of Arnold's novel. Its art is uninspired. What matters is the notable qualities of mind it reveals. Arnold shares a characteristic habit of the Victorian liberal : he approaches social problems in terms too purely moral. His hero, Edward Oakfield, is a moral hero, like George Eliot's Felix Holt who is meant to be a Radical but elevates the purely moral above the social. Still, the intelligent liberals are able to see the problems themselves, though not the 'solutions', with unusual penetration. Of course, Arnold is far more of a moral reformer than George Eliot. All his important characters are highly moral themselves and over moralists, as in the case of Oakfield, Hugh Stanton and Mr. Middleton, or they soon develop into such people, as do Arthur Vernon and Freed Wykham. Oakfield, in fact, is religious-minded, and comes to India to find fulfilment :

> In the colonies—in a new, fresh, and vigorous society, he thought form would, at any rate, weigh less heavily upon truth ; society if it did not help, would surely not hinder him. In this direction he was met by practical difficulties at all hands ; till at last, transferring his notions of colonial to Anglo-Indian society, with an ignorance marvellous indeed, but common to all Englishmen not connected by family ties with India, he fancied he had solved the problem—that by obtaining an Indian appointment a maintenance would be secured to him, while he, under utterly new circumstances, might begin life anew, try once more to realize his theory of bringing religion into daily life, without the necessity of denying it at every turn in obedience to some fashion or dogma of society ; and then, as to his work in life, was not every European in India engaged in the grand work of civilizing Asia ?[4]

Arnold attributes Oakfield's notions of Anglo-Indian society to a common 'ignorance'. He thus virtually states their falsity, suggests his objective view of his hero and a part of his own stance, knowledgeable realism. He proceeds to expose diverse aspects of Anglo-Indian society mainly in terms of Oakfield's awakening to them. 'The overbearing coarse animal worldly existence'[5] of the Anglo-Indians, as he sees it, is bodied forth concretely during Oakfield's assignments in two regiments—the 81st regiment at Hajeepoor, whose evils at their worst are represented by Lieutenant Cade, and a less reprehensible, different kind of regiment, the 90th, whose weakness at their worst are represented by Stafford. Oakfield finds army society less uncongenial during the war with the Sikhs because of its 'physical earnestness, although he still sought in vain, and still regretted the absence of that moral earnestness which should give its character to war as to everything else'.[6] As a reward for courageous military service, he is appointed to the civil service in Punjab and thus Arnold opens up another side of Anglo-India. This is Oakfield's reaction to it :

> I like it better than I expected, or rather dislike it less.[7]

Take the majority of officials in this country : their vigour, their strong sense, their prompt and business-like dexterity, have earned for them as a class, a justly honourable distinction. These are what may be called the commercial virtues. But except good men of business what are they ?[8]

As E.M. Forster thinks, the novel 'has the Arnold integrity'.[9] Its brave and knowledgeable exposure of Anglo-India in mid-Victorian times has a value. William Arnold's view of it is sombre ; consider the fates of his worthy central characters : at the end of the novel, Stanton and Middleton are inclined to quit India, Wykham goes to England on furlough and decides against return, Vernon and Oakfield himself are unable to come to terms with Anglo-India and contract fatal illnesses. In the face of Anglo-India which they regarded as more or less unsatisfactory, these characters had become friends and this helped to keep alive 'the chords of their finer nature'. 'Fellowship', as the sub-title has it, is important to Arnold as it is to Forster, but Arnold is concerned only with the Europeans.

This pre-occupation suggests the boundaries of his view of India. He pays most attention to life in the army. And, indeed, the army does bulk large in literature set in places subject to imperailism : apart from Kipling, military contributions were prominent in *Blackwood's Edinburgh Magazine* which became staple reading for army officers, planters, administrative officials, and other members of the imperial service and was the usual magazine for which they wrote.[10] This interest reflects the importance of the army in gaining empires, and extending and maintaining them ; when Frantz Fanon says that colonialism 'is violence in its natural state,'[11] he is stating part of the truth.

To turn now to the role of the Indians in Arnold's novel's

on the social relations of British Soldiers, Edward Oakfield says in conversation with Miss Middleton :

'Beyond our official connexion with the sepoys, and our domestic relations with our servants, we see really nothing of the people, have nothing to do with them, no influence, nor any opportunity of gaining influence with them.'

'I dare say,' said Miss Middleton, 'that that is quite true ; intercourse with the natives is just one of those vague sweeping expressions which the people in England are so fond of with regard to India.'[12]

When Oakfield serves in the army, he is very friendly with a British civil servant, Middleton, but he is not even acquainted with a single Indian inside or outside the army. Even when he himself becomes a civil servant, he remains aloof from the Indians. The Indians themselves appear only briefly in the novel, as servants and bearers of palkis ; none of them is individualized ; none of them speaks a word. Because of the prevailing apartheid, they do not matter in the area of European social life which Arnold has chosen to depict. His presentation is true to his selected area, but it is narrow.

Yet Arnold is not wholly unconcerned with the kind of relations between the races which was to pre-occupy Forster in *A Passage to India.* There is this conversation of Oakfield's with Wykham at Simla :

'Well, I do detest the natives, they are a mean, lying, fawning, sordid race ; and after ten years experience, I say that to call a native "a man and a brother" is a lie. He is not a man ; and I repudiate the fraternity of a scoundrel who lies at every other word'.

'My experience is much less than yours, and I grant you their lying is most awful ; but then this is just one of the evils which I say weigh upon us in this country. It is grievous to live among men, and feel the idea of fraternity thwarted by facts ; and yet the idea must not be abandoned as false or hopeless. We must not resign ourselves, without a struggle, to calling them brutes.'[13]

Wykham is an utter racialist, but it is the less superior Oakfield who has Arnold behind him. Oakfield goes on to say :

"We esteem them the better, the more we know them. Why ? because we learn to look at things from their view, instead of assuming our own as the true one, and condemning them for not coming up to it."[14]

He wishes to remove the distinctions of colour and language, and to achieve 'a growing sense of unity'.[15] But the 'unity' he advocates is between a superior 'white' race and an inferior race which has somehow got rid of its inferiority :

'But after all, I grant freely that they are a deplorably inferior race, but I do not see why they should be considered hopelessly so.'[16]

Thus Arnold rises above the characteristically imperial attitudes of Wykham, but he makes the traditional Western mistake of confusing a less developed state of culture with an alleged inferiority of race.

But Arnold and Oakfield are not 'the same person', as Forster takes them to be.[17] Arnold does endorse his hero's views to a considerable extent, but he also differs from him at times. Apart from explicit criticism, Arnold also uses a less obvious method of implicit criticism, which is evident when Middleton sketches his idea of India's progress to Oakfield and Mr. Wallace :

"To preach Christianity to the natives of India, is to begin at the end. Physical improvement first, then intellectual, then spiritual, that seems the natural order of things ; and if it is the natural order, that is to say the true one, fixed by the laws of the universe, then whole universities of missionaries will not alter it.[18]

It is the practical, experienced Middleton whose attitudes Arnold shows up as always sound. He is Arnold's mouthpiece rather than Oakfield. By playing off their characters, he implicitly 'places' Oakfield as an over-moral idealist. 'The natural order of things', to which Arnold subscribes, is sensible. But he cannot escape the limitations of traditional attitudes : he tends to equate the 'spiritual' with the religious, considers Christianity necessary for India and sees all improvement a work of the

British. This exchange between Oakfield and Middleton is also important :

'But do you not contemplate a time when this government shall pass into the people's own hands ?

'Surely ; I do contemplate it, but I confess, as an infinitely remote event, of which, at present, it is I think impossible to detect any, the faintest symptom. The grand fault in our government has been and is, that it does not contemplate this, and does not therefore try to find out the causes which at present make it so utterly unfeasible.'[19]

As early as 1853, Arnold can look upon self-rule as a worthy and neglected goal in India ; at that time it would naturally appear 'an infinitely remote event' even to him. But Middleton sees the two key problems in these terms ; 'What is the point at which the European and the Native mind begin to diverge ?' 'Why is English society in this country so woefully behind all European society elsewhere ?'[20] Then he gives his own 'solution' :

'The solution of a problem like that can hardly be stated categorically ; it is the work of our lives of yours and mine, to solve it ; or rather to make some approach to it, for he who really does solve it will be the great man of India. The solution of it will be a revelation made to us by some man of genius ; the great business for ordinary honest workers is pioneering, trying to clear away some of the jungle of falsehood and absurdity which might stop the hero or impede him, when he does come.'[21]

The positive 'approach' is absurdly visionary.

Arnold reveals the strength of an exceptional mid-Victorian liberal : he is courageously honest, sees problems realistically and can transcend common prejudices. But he is limited by conventional thought and by his period to a certain extent. The wishful and over-moral side of his mind belongs to the weak side of the liberal tradition : his brother, Matthew, keenly grasped the problems of contemporary England but adumbrated inadequate solutions.[22] Of George Eliot, David Craig has written : '. . . . all George Eliot can offer, through Felix, is high-mindedness, unrooted in any particular activity or movement.'[23]

Both *Oakfield* and Knighton's *Forest Life in Ceylon* are rooted in actual experience and information. But in latter the dividing line between fact and art is thin, and it is not organized into a unified novel. I think it is best approached in terms of the author's own conception of his work, 'a collection of light sketches professing to describe life.'[24] What strikes me as valuable in it is his exceptionally intelligent contemplation of colonial situations in Ceylon in mid-Victorian times :

'There is much in an Asiatic life generally,' observed Hofer, 'that tends to unfit a man for active duties in England afterwards; here, and more especially on the continent of India, a man begins naturally to regard himself as one of the aristocracy, however, humble his lot at home. He sees the great mass of the population beneath him, its chiefs solicitous for his friendship or notice, and a favoured few of the same rank and class with himself enjoying a monopoly of the advantages of life. It is therefore but natural that he should begin to esteem himself as a very different being from the common herd of humanity around him—as a portion of China amongst the earthenware of the world . . . .'[25]

On the other hand, there is little of this intelligence in his pondered comments on the 'rebellion' soon after the British conquest of Kandy, the last stronghold of the Sinhalese :

'United the Kandians might possibly at this juncture have succeeded in again achieving independence, although I cannot agree with Marandhan in thinking that such a consummation would have ultimately been for the good of the country, but, distracted by dissension, and divided by clashing interests and pretensions all hope of ultimate success was foolish.'

'The second was that invariable good fortune, which makes the British advance in the East the march of destiny, which no accident can arrest, no temporary losses retard.'[26]

His confident views are conventional, especially the notion of 'the British advance' as a matter of 'destiny'.[27] He is not as far-seeing as William Arnold.

Nevertheless, when he sets himself the straight-forward task of describing his journey by pilot-boat after his ship has entered the Galle harbour, he is capable of remarkable honesty :

To my unsophisticated eyes, the crew of this boat appeared to be tame monkeys. So completely was my conception of humanity mixed up with clothes and white or black skins, that it was, for a time, impossible for me to realize to myself the idea that these gibbering, long-armed, brown, naked animals were fellow-creatures. Even now, after having had many years' experience of the East, I still believe that more unfavourable specimens of the natives of Ceylon could scarcely have been met with than those in the boat. Three of them were old men, their ribs too distinguishable through their leather-like skin, their arms dry and shrivelled ; yet their advanced age was not to be seen at once—their long, bony, and muscular arms, deprived of every particle of fat ; their fingers rendered remarkable by the white nails at the tips ; the palms of their hands white from constant labour ; and the contrast between their brown, shrivelled-up wrinkled skins, and the scanty white or blue cloth which they wore round their loins, all formed a picture so like that which a party of tamed monkeys would present, that it was not without disgust I gazed at them—disgust, mingled with something of indignation, that these animals should be of the same species as myself. Nor did the grizzled beards, and the bare shaggy heads, from which they had removed their straw fishermen's hats, tend to improve the picture, or make them more human-like. My feelings were shared by my companions, and, as we muttered to each other, 'These are the natives', we could not help wondering how humanity could degenerate into such figures ; forgetting that the want of dress and difference of colour were the only real points of contrast between them and similar specimens of our own countrymen.[28]

Knighton's candour, though naive, is valuable. His observations, say of the 'leather-like skin' and 'arms dry and shrivelled' of the Sinhalese crew, is keen. On later reflection, he is sensible enough to realize 'that the want of dress and difference of colour were the only real points of contrast between them and similar specimens of our own countrymen', to self-critically diagnose racialism. It happens again in his account of dinner at an hotel ashore :

Nor was it without a feeling of unpleasantness that I saw my plate handed about by the dark fingers—a transient feeling, which I distinctly remember having once felt, but which must very soon have passed away with use.[29]

Observe the characteristic frankness and the living detail of the incident. Though Knighton is not as far-seeing as Arnold, his writing has more verve and immediacy : it is more closely and specifically rooted in his colonial context. Whereas Arnold's moral view was formed before his Indian experience and was applied to it as it would be to any other, Knighton's broadening outlook arises out of his Ceylon experience and is being shaped by it. He is more alive in his alien setting, and this is one reason why he can bring into his sketches a 'native', Marandhan, as an important and respect-worthy person.

William Arnold and Knighton are immediate forerunners of Conrad, Kipling, Forster, Joyce Cary, and Graham Greene, on the one hand, and of Mulk Raj Anand, R. K. Narayan, Chinua Achebe, James Ngugi and V.S. Naipaul, on the other. It was colonial officials such as they who set up the tradition which leads to these writers of literature in English about situations in the Third World.

NOTES

1. Benjamin Kidd, *The Control of the Tropics*, London & New York, 1898, p. 65.
2. See John F. Bayliss, 'Slave and Convict Narratives : A Discussion of American and Australian Writing', *JCL*, 8.
3. For instance, Roscoe's *The Wrongs of Africa*, 1787.
4. William Delafied Arnold, *Oakfield or Fellowship in the East*, 1853, Vol. I, p. 16.
5. Ibid., Vol. I, pp. 69-70.
6. Ibid., Vol. II, p. 57.
7. Ibid., Vol. II, p. 219.
8. Ibid, Vol. 24, p. 224.
9. E. M. Forster, William Arnold', *Two Cheers for Democracy*, 1965 edn., p. 204.

10. For instance, in *Blackwood's Edinburgh Magazine*, November 1899 (Vol. CLXVI) : Capt. Neil Malcolm, 'On Service in the Uganda Protectorate', and Gen. Sir Henry Brackenbury, 'The Transvaal Twenty Years Ago' ; and January 1893 (Vol. CLIII) : Archer P. Crouch, 'The French in West Africa'.
11. Frantz Fanon, *The Wretched of the Earth*, 1967 edn., p. 48.
12. *Oakfield*, Vol. II, p. 254.
13. Ibid., Vol. II, p. 138.
14. Ibid Vol. II, p. 140.
15. Ibid., Vol. II, p. 141.
16. Ibid., Vol. II, p. 141.
17. E.M. Forster, op. cit., p. 201.
18. *Oakfield*, Vol. I, p. 189.
19. Ibid., Vol. I, pp. 168-9.
20. Ibid., Vol. I, pp. 170-171.
21. Ibid., Vol. I, p. 180.
22. In his essay 'Equality (*Mixed Essays*), he responds delicately and humanely to 'the great inequality of classes and property' ; but politics is to him mere machinery and turbulence.
23. David Craig, 'Fiction and the Rising Industrial Classes', *Essays in Criticism*, XVII, I (1967), p. 69.
24. William Knighton, *Forest Life In Ceylon*, 1854, Vol. II, p. 361.
25. Ibid., Vol. II, p. 69.
26. Ibid., Vol. II, p. 249.
27. For similar views, see W. Arnold, 'Preface', *Oakfield*, p. ix.
28. *Forest Life in Ceylon*, Vol. I, pp. 7-8.
29. Ibid., Vol. I, p. 20.

CHAPTER 7

Colonial Neuroses : Kipling and Forster

Margery Perham, the distinguished authority on colonial affairs, has spoken of her feelings when she was about to enter Somaliland for the first time :

> Next day we were to cross the Gulf of Aden to Berbera to live almost alone and far inland among a population of dark people. I had an overwhelming spasm of recoil, of something more than physical fear. I referred to this in one of my Reith Lectures : a revulsion against the thought that I, so white, so vulnerable, so sensitive, so complex, was about to commit myself to that continent across the water, one among tens of thousands of strange, dark, fierce, uncomprehending people, and live away on that far frontier, utterly cut off from my own race. It was like a nightmare. I suppose it was racial fear. It passed.[1]

This kind of nightmarish experience was a characteristic aspect of European life in the colonies, and I propose to examine its presence in Kipling's earliest stories and Forster's *A Passage to India.* Probably, "racial fear" is only a part of this experience ; the cultural fear of the alien and the invaders' fear of their subjects[2] are more or less important causes.

It is natural that this aspect of colonial life should have occupied Kipling's mind at the beginning of his literary career just as it was a part of Conrad's concers in his first two (Malayan) novels and in his African tales. Louis L. Cornell argues that Kipling's four earliest stories were "a false start and that it was through newspaper sketches, not grotesque tales, that the main course of his development was to lie."[3] But it seems to me that "the main course of his development" was only partly through "newspaper sketches"; it *was* partly through these stories of nightmarish experience that he arrived at the body of his work, which focused on the ordinary world of Anglo-India. The development of Kipling's interest from nightmarish experience to ordinary experience is logical : he moves from a kind of colonial experience which tends to strike a sensitive alien like Margery Perham, Conrad or himself with immediate force, to experience which impinges later on the consciousness of such a person. Moreover, Cornell's epithet, "grotesque," does not accurately describe the earliest stories of Kipling.

There are more reasons why these stories are an integral part of Kipling's development as an artist, reasons which effect their quality. These stories illustrate the kind of unevenness despite consistent care which, W.W. Robson observes, is one feature of Kipling's work at any period of his career.[4] In all of them Kipling, like Conrad, employed narrators partly for the sake of an objectivity which became characteristic and a condition of artistic success, though it did not consistently guarantee it in his case. These stories reveal his type of economy. This probably derives mainly from his habit, as he himself confesses in his autobiography, of "shortening his Anglo-Indian tales, first to his own fancy after rapturous re-readings and next to the space available"[5]—that is, a habit formed by considerations of artistic effect and journalistic exigence.[6] His fictive economy at times contributes to and at other times detracts from the power of his stories ; these stories about nightmarish experiences are no exception. In "The Gate of the Hundred Sorrows" (1884), he treats Gabral Misquitta's opium-addiction as the centre of the story, but he artfully introduces a compressed account of Misquitta's entire life to bring out the full import of his deterioration. But in "The Dream of Duncan Parrenness" (1884) he condenses too much. The story is an allegory about a European's maturation after a nightmare, set in India in the eighteenth century when Warren Hastings was Governor-General :

> Yet there be certain times in a young man's life, when, through great sorrow of sin, all the boy in him is burnt and seared away so that he passes at one step to the more sorrowful state of manhood : as our staring Indian day

changes into night with never so much as the grey of twilight to temper the two extremes.[7]

This extremely swift maturation passes through three stages : Parrenness's future self takes from him his "trust in man," his "faith in women" and as much as remained to him of his "boy's soul and conscience."[8] The whole process is rendered with an extreme conciseness which is partly responsible for the impression of slickness created by the development of the action.

The basic narrative mode of all these stories is the same and is that which was established in *Blackwood's Edinburgh Magazine*[9]—that of the "sahib" recounting his experiences in the colonies. But the quality of the language in each and also the quality of the experiences, though all are broadly nightmarish, are diverse. As a Eurasian deteriorating in a colony, Misquitta in "The Gate of the Hundred Sorrows" is a representative figure and belongs with such characters as Conrad's Almayer and Willems, Joyce Cary's Gollup in *Mister Johnson.*

> How did I take to it ? It began at Calcutta. I used to try it in my own house, just to see what it was like. I never went very far, but I think my wife must have died then. Anyhow, I found myself here, and got to know Fung-Tching. I don't remember rightly how that came about : but he told me of the Gate and I used to go there, and, somehow, I have never got away from it since. Mind you, though, the Gate was a respectable place in Fung-Tching's time, where you could be comfortable and not at all like the *chandookhanas* where the niggers go. No ; it was clean, and quiet, and not crowded. Of course, there were others beside us ten and the man ; but we always had a mat apiece, with a wadded woollen headpiece, all covered with black and red dragons and things, just like the coffin in corner.
>
> At the end of one's third pipe the dragons used to move about and fight. I've watched 'em many and many a night through. I used to regulate my Smoke that way, and now it takes a dozen pipes to make 'em stir. Besides, they are all torn and dirty, like the mats, and old Fung Tching is dead.[10]

An "I" introduces the story at the beginning as that told entirely by Misquitta when he was at death's door. As the story unfolds itself, it becomes clear that Misquitta had become fatally addicted to opium. At this point, he is halfway through his account when Kipling introduces one of his flashbacks to an earlier period of Misquitta's life. It coheres with the rest as a natural part of one of his open answers to the "I's" series of implied questions, answers which compose the whole story. This flashback is one of his rather hazy recollections of the origins of his addiction which the reader finds suggestive. Throuh it Kipling shows Misquitta's deterioration in depth and, at the same time, ensures that the story is unfailingly in character. On the other hand, it is equally appropriate that Misquitta describes precisely the stage of opium addiction because it comes later and grips his mind : evokes the very experience of the increased addiction to opium-smoking. Through this kind of conversational idiom, Kipling presents Misquitta's case from the addict's standpoint as well as implies his own through suggestions in the language and organization beyond the narrator's consciousness. Here Kipling suggests how Misquitta's fate is of his own making though he does not face this squarely, how he clings incongruously to his sense of superiority as a sahib when both his character and his opium den have declined. The deterioration of the den parallels and intensifies his own. Kipling uses Misquitta's expression of happiness over his poor allowance of "sixty rupees fresh and fresh every month" as a kind of refrain which suggests an abortive attempt to appease a nagging sense failure beneath his protestations of contentment and indifference. His last hopes are in keeping with and suggest movingly the irretrievable wreck which he has become :

> One of these days, I hope, I shall die in the Gate . . . . I should like to die like the bazar-woman—on a clean, cool mat with a pipe of good stuff between my lips. When I feel I'm going, I shall ask Tsing-ling for them, and he can draw my sixty rupees a month, fresh and fresh, as long as he pleases. Then I shall lie back, quiet and comfortable, and watch the black and red dragons have their last big fight

together ; and then . . . . Well, it doesn't matter. Nothing matters much to me—only I wish Tsing-ling wouldn't put bran into the Black Smoke.[11]

Not all the nightmarish experiences of Europeans in colonies, however, arise because of or are conditioned by that complex of colonial fears which I mentioned at the beginning. The young Kipling realized this. The "dream" of Duncan Parrenness is couched in an archaic prose to suit its period, but it remains rather artificially sterile. The dream remains artistically flimsy and is not related to those colonial fears. In "The Phanton Rickshaw" (1885), a much better story than "The Dream of Duncan Parrenness," Kipling subtly suggests that Jack Pansay's "delusion" reflects a kind of schizophrenia caused mainly by his sense of guilt over his affair with Mrs. Keith-Wessington. It is not presented as an experience which is typically or specially colonial.

Yet in "The Strange Ride of Morrowbie Jukes" (1885), Kipling presents a colonial kind of experience, "going native," which appears nightmarish to a sahib. The sahib, Jukes, narrates his own story and the author introduces it. The author vouches for its truth, but indicates that Jukes "has touched it up in places and introduced Moral Reflections"[12] presumably from his present healthy and maturer state in ordinary Anglo-India. The latter point is clear in the story, but the former is qualified by the story itself. Jukes is, certainly, true to his experience, but the experience itself is half fantasy. The authorities of the Village of the Dead remain mystery and the armed boat, which guards the only almost totally unknown way of escape from the Village through the swamp, is inexplicably rather strange. But these are suitable correlatives for Jukes's nightmarish experience—of being ruthlessly hemmed in by "native" life and of inner discomposure because of an overturning of his notion of what social roles should be and were in a colony. The European as conqueror holds the "native" in subjection basically through force which appears nakedly during "rebellion," but here the roles are reversed :

> As I led Pornic over the sands I was startled by the faint pop of a rifle across the river ; and at the same moment a bullet dropped with a sharp '*whit*' close to Pornic's head.
>
> There was no mistaking the nature of the missile—a regulation Martini-Henry 'picket'. About five hundred yards away a country-boat was anchored in mid-stream ; and a jet of smoke drifting away from its bows in the still morning air showed me whence the delicate attention had come. Was ever a respectable gentleman in such an *impasse* ? The treacherous sand-slope allowed no escape from a spot which I had visited most involuntarily, and a promenade on the river frontage was the signal for a bombardment from some insane native in a boat. I'm afraid I lost my temper very much indeed. Another bullet reminded me that I had better save my breath to cool my porridge . . . . (p. 138).

Kipling captures the kind of slightly forced playfulness which a sahib would come out with in this kind of situation, and the shooting is described exactly. The fantasy works because it stylises into an extreme form the actual essence of the coloniser's position.

Jukes's experience is half real in an extremely grim way. He has to live among Hindu outcasts on the verge of death in a tiny barren village in a crater. He has no alternative but to live on a staple diet of crows and sleep in a filthy hole in a sand-bank. Thus he is placed in extremely primitive and difficult circumstances which test the very essentials of his kind of character. Kipling renders ironically a range of feelings within Jukes arising from a tension between his ingrained sense of superiority as "a Sahib, a representative of the dominant race" (p. 144), which is absurd for one in his situation, and a sense of inescapable degradation.

> One does not protest against the doings of a den of wild beasts ; and my companions were lower than any beasts. While I ate what Gunga Dass had provided, a coarse *chapatti* and a cupful of the foul well-water, the people showed not the faintest sign of curiosity—that curiosity which is so rampant, as a rule, in an Indian village.

> I could even fancy that they despised me. At all events they treated me with the most chilling indifference, and Gunga Dass was nearly as bad. I plied him with questions about the terrible village, and received extremely unsatisfactory answers. (p. 143)

Jukes's experience is brought to a focus mainly through his interaction with Gunga Dass. He had known the Indian earlier as a Government servant with among other things "unctuous speech" (p. 139) But Dass now treats him differently. Indeed, none of the Hindus place him on his accustomed sahib's pedestal. His case is in some ways similar to and in others different from Dass's. The latter feels that his present state is a humiliation particularly because he is conscious of his past as a "Brahmin and a proud man" (p. 141), as a high caste and a proud man. He reconciles himself with difficulty to life in the Village, but Jukes finds it impossible to do this. The difference in their positions in Anglo-India matters here. The perils which await a person such as Jukes are indicated concretely when he learns of the Englishman who had died there and sees his remains. These carefully woven significances arise from the action whose realistic aspect, like its fantastic one, is rendered in precise detail. This is equally true of the everyday activities such as eating, and of the social attitudes that come up. It brings the story potently to the senses so that we lose the sense that it is half fantasy. Indeed, it raises it to the level of a symbolic dramatisation of aspects of "ruling-race" and "native" psychology in a colony.

In *A Passage to India*, Forster also deals with the subject of colonial neurosis. In this respect, Adela Quested and Mrs. Moore in the Marabar Caves have physical, psychological and cultural affinities with Jukes in the crater. The visit to the Caves is the crux of the whole action, and their nightmarish experiences during and after it are an important part of the novel's significance. Adela imagines that Aziz had tried to rape her in a cave. Forster suggests that Aziz did not do so, but he leaves vague what actually happened to Adela in there. The question as to what happened is as irrelevant as "How many children had Lady Macbeth ?" What matters is that in a situation of social and racial friction there can be no smoke without fire. The British and the Indians gather as though they were opposed armies, as Forster suggests in the novel.[13] The British as alien invaders feel a nightmarish sense of beleaguerment :

> People drove into the club with studious calm—the jog trot of country gentlefolk between green hedgerows, for the natives must not suspect that they were agitated. They exchange the usual drinks, but everything tasted different and then they looked out at the palisade of cactuses stabbing the purple throat of the sky ; they realized that they were thousands of miles from any scenery that they understood. (pp. 177-78).

Forster metaphorically suggests that even nature seems to them murderously menacing because they have projected their own kind of fear onto it. Adela herself is haunted by a echo after her experience, in the cave, and this is a definite sign of neurosis. The echo disappears after she clears Aziz of the charge, and this suggests that it is associated in her unconscious mind partly with a doubt as to his culpability and a related sense of guilt, a sense that she has brought the experience on herself.

Thus Forster is able to render the nightmarish kind of experience of Europeans in colonies with a psychological and social depth which Kipling achieves in the best of his earliest stories, "The Strange Ride of Morrowble Jukes." Yet Forster also sees a philosophical dimension to this kind of experience which the young Kipling does not. The Marabar Caves themselves are important in this respect :

> The first cave was tolerably convenient. They skirted the puddle of water, and then climbed up over some unattractive stones, the sun crashing on their backs. Bending their heads, they disappeared one by one into the interior of the hills. The small black hole gaped where their varied forms and colours had momentarily functioned. They were sucked in like water down a drain. Bland and bold rose the precipices ; bland and glutinous the sky that connected the precipices ;

> solid and white, a Brahminy kite flapped between the rocks with a clumsiness that seemed intentional. Before man, with his itch for the seemly, had been born, the planet must have looked thus. The kite flapped away . . . . Before birds, perhaps . . . And then the hole belched and humanity returned. (pp. 144-45)

Nature is presented accurately and strikingly in terms of human reactions to it, and is linked to the human action. Forster unobtrusively introduces symbolic suggestions of life as being puny in a world which has come to pass through a long mindless evolution ; the sense of the material world as "viscous" as so much clogging stuff devoid of values, anticipates Sartre. Suggestions of this kind begin to converge on Mrs. Moore. It is mainly through her that Forster presents his deepest insights into philosophical rather than social matters.

> A Marabar cave had been horrid as far as Mrs. Moore was concerned, for she had nearly fainted in it, and had some difficulty in preventing herself from saying so as soon as she got into the air again. It was natural enough : she had always suffered from faintness, and the cave had become too full, because all their retinue followed them. Crammed with villagers and servants, the circular chamber began to smell. She lost Aziz in the dark, didn't know who touched her, couldn't breathe, and some vile naked thing struck her face and settled on her mouth like a pad. She tried to regain the entrance tunnel, but an influx of villagers swept her back. She hit her head. For an instant she went mad, hitting and gasping like a fanatic. For not only did the crush and stench alarm her ; there was also a terrifying echo.
>
> Professor Godbole had never mentioned an echo ; it never impressed him, perhaps. (p. 145)

It is a European, not an Indian, who is prone to have experiences of this kind. On a realistic level, Forster renders the reactions of an elderly European woman. At the same time, he suggests symbolically a surreal sense of the unreality of the world of fact.

> There are some exquisite echoes in India ; there is the whisper round the dome at Bijapur ; there are the long, solid sentences that voyage through the air at Mandhu, and return unbroken to their creator. The echo in a Marabar cave is not like these, it is entirely devoid of distinction. Whatever is said, the same monotonous noise replies, and quivers up and down the walls until it is absorbed into the roof, 'Boum' is the sound as far as the human alphabet can express it, or 'bou-oum' or 'ou-boum',—utterly dull. Hope, politeness, the blowing of a nose, the squeak of a boot, all produce 'boum'. (p. 145).

It echo is real and, at the same time a recurring symbol of a sense of nullity. It goes with that sense of life as being puny, and these two kinds of symbolism intensify each other.

> The crush and the smells she could forget, but the echo began in some indescribable way to undermine her hold on life. Coming at a moment when she chanced to be fatigued, it had managed to murmur, 'Pathos, piety, courage—they exist, but are identical, and so is filth. Everything exists, nothing has value.' If one had spoken vileness in that place, or quoted lofty poetry, the comment would have been the same —'ou-boum'. If one had spoken with the tongues of angels and pleaded for all the unhappiness and misunderstanding in the world, past, present, and to come, for all the misery men must undergo whatever their opinion and position, and however much they dodge or bluff—it would amount to the same, the serpent would descend and return to the ceiling. Devils are of the North, and poems can be written about them, but no one could romanticize the Marabar because it robbed infinity and eternity of their vastness, the only quality that accommodates them to mankind. (p. 147).

For an instant the prose here deteriorates into false rhetoric ("Devils are of the North and poems can be written about them") ; devils are found in the mythology of cultures at least as far south as Ceylon and Bali. This apart, the nullity and pettiness of life are presented with power and particularity. It is an outstanding characteristic of this phase of the novel that the real and the symbolic interpenetrate, and Forster thereby success in the difficult task of rendering philosophical considerations with the concreteness of immediate experience. From one aspect Mrs. Moore reflects the depressed sense of an absence of solidly accepted or acceptable system of values which haunts the modern European mind. In this respect Forster is in the line from Hardy (for instance, *Jude the Obscure*) and Nietzsche "(God is dead. God remains dead. And we killed him."), through to existentialism and the Absurd (for instance, Beckett's *Waiting for Godot*).

Mrs. Moore's wisdom is appreciated neither by the British nor by the Indians. Adela thinks that "the old lady had turned disagreeable and queer" after the episode at the Caves (p. 212). Aziz is attached to her emotionally, but she is "nothing" to him in an intellectual sense (p. 307). Her apotheosis as "Esmiss Esmoor" by the mass of the Indians reflects a spontaneous religious reaction, which primitive. She is presented by Forster with a critical realism. We noticed that her elderliness matters ; here is a part of the scene immediately after her experience in the cave :

> As each person emerged she looked for a villain, cut none was there, and she realized that she had been among the mildest individuals, whose only desire was to honour her, and that the naked pad was a poor little baby, astride its mother'ship. Nothing evil had been in the cave, but she had not enjoyed herself ; no, she had not enjoyed herself, and she decided not to visit a second one. (p. 146)

Forster suggests that she had made too much of her experience. Here she is leaving India :

> As she drove through the huge city which the West had built and abandoned with a gesture of despair, she longed to stop, though it was only Bombay, and disentangle the hundred Indias that passed each other in its streets. The feet of the horses moved her on, and presently the boat sailed and thousands of coconut palms appeared all round the anchorage and climbed the hills to wave her farewell. 'So you thought an echo was India ; you took the Marabar caves as final ?'

> they laughed. 'What have we in common with them, or they with Asirgarh ? Good-bye !' (pp. 204-5)

Forster suggests that it is because Mrs. Moore is an outsider that she finds it impossible to understand India, though he is aware that it is an extremely complex country. Her view is deeper than the conventional "mysterious-East" kind of view, but is still limited. Mrs. Moore's character is a development from Mrs. Wilcox's in *Howards End*, but unlike Mrs. Wilcox, she comes alive as both fully real and richly symbolic. The nightmarish kind of experiences of Europeans in colonies provide one way by which Forster is able to make a "passage to more than India" (to use Walt Whitman's phrase). He taps the same vein as the young Kipling ; yet he attempts and achieves a much larger structure of experiences and significances than the latter.

NOTES

1. Margery Perham, "African Dreams" *The Listener*, 12 March, 1970, p. 336.
2. This is evident, for example, in Churchill's speeches on India : When the nation finds that whole position is in jeopardy, that her whole work and duty in India is being brought to a standstill, when the nation sees our individual fellow-countrymen scattered about, with their women and children, through this enormous land, in hourly peril amidst the Indian multitudes, when at any moment, this may produce shocking scenes, then I think there will be a sharp awakening, then, I am sure, that a reaction of the most vehement character will sweep this country and its unmeasured strength will once more be used. That, Sir, is an ending which I trust and pray we may avoid, but it is an ending to which, step by step and day by day, we are being remorselessly and fatuously conducted.—Winston S. Churchill. *India* : *Speeches* (London : T. Butterworth, 1931), p. 69.
3. Louis L. Cornell, *Kipling in India* (New York : St. Martin's Press, 1966), p. 108.

4. W. W. Robson, "Kipling's Later Stories," in *Kipling's Mind and Art*, ed. Andrew Rutherford (Edinburgh & London : Oliver & Boyd, 1965), p. 258.
5. Kipling, *Something of Myself* (London : Macmillan, 1964), p. 207.
6. For instance, "thirty-two of the *Plain Tales* had been printed in the *Civil and Military* ; the remaining eight made their first appearance when the book was published, in January 1888" : Charles Carrington, *Rudyard Kipling : His Life and Work* (London : Penguin, 1970), p. 129.
7. Kipling, "The Dream of Duncan Parrenness," *Life's Handicap* (London : Macmillan, 1964), p. 302.
8. Ibid., pp. 300, 301.
9. See, e.g. Sir Hugh Clifford, "The Quest of the Golden Fleece," '*Blackwood*' *Tales from the Outposts* (Edinburgh & London : William Blackwood, 1933), Vol. 8 ; Lord Baden-Powell, "Jokilobovu," ibid., Vol. 9 ; J.A.G. Elliot, "The Ngoloko," ibid., Vol. 9 ; Lieut-Colonel R.L. Kennion, "A Country Postman," ibid., Vol. 1 ; Lieut-Colonel F.M. Bailey, "A Quiet Day in Tibet," ibid., Vol. 1.
10. Kipling, 'The Gate of the Hundred Sorrows' : *Plain Tales from the Hills* (London : Macmillan, 1964), pp. 215-16.
11. Ibid., p. 218.
12. Kipling, "The Strange Ride of Morrowbie Jukes," *Wee Willie Winkie* (London : Macmillian, 1964), p. 134 ; all later quotations from the story are from this editions and their page-numbers are noted in my text.
13. Forster, *A Passage to India* (London : Penguin, 1959), p. 167; all quotations from the novel are from this edition and their page-numbers are noted in my text.

CHAPTER 8

Kipling's Indian Poetry

In his earliest stories ("The Gate of the Hundred sorrows" "The Dream of Duncan Parrenness", "The Phantom Rickshaw" and "The Strange Ride of Morrowbie Jukes"), Kipling deals with nightmarish experiences of Europeans in colonies and he is free of imperialist attitudes. But when we consider the work in which he contemplates relationships between British and Indians in the ordinary world of Anglo-India, we ought to grasp how extremely difficult it was at that time for an Englishman to get beyond the mental habits of his people, whether he was based in England or in India. For this was the age of Joseph Chamberlain and Cecil Rhodes, and today views such as theirs are hard to imagine :

> In the first place, I believe in the British Empire and, in the second place, I believe in the British race. I believe that the British race is the greatest of governing races that the world has ever seen. (Chamberlain)[1]

> I admit that we have made mistakes. I have no doubt that we are answerable for sins of commission as well as for sins of omission ; but, after all is said, this remains—that we alone among the nations of the earth have been able to establish and to maintain colonies under different conditions in all parts of the world, that we have maintained them to their own advantage and to ours, and that we have secured, not only the loyal attachment of all British subjects, but the general goodwill of the races, whether they be native or whether they be European, that have thus come under the British flag. (Chamberlain)[2]

> We are the first race in the world, and, more of the world we inhabit, the better it is for the human race. (Rhodes)[3]

In India colonial sentiments, including racialism, appeared unmistakably during the storm over the Ilbert Bill (1882) which sought to put Europeans on the same legal footing as Indians. European agitation compelled the Viceroy, Lord Ripon, to draft a compromise whereby Europeans could ask for a jury half of whose members were of their own race. The British were thus anxious to maintain their racial identity in the colonial environment.

It is in relation to imperial matters such as these that I propose to discuss briefly Kipling's Indian poetry. Let us begin with the early poems. It has been pointed out that the notorious line from "The Ballad of East and West" (1889)—

> Oh, East is East, and West is West, and never the twain shall meet—

is followed by

> But there is neither East nor West, Border, nor Breed, nor Birth,
>
> When two strong men stand face to face, though they come from the ends of the earth.[4]

This may look like evidence of an absence of racialism in Kipling as Jack Dunman and M. Tarinayya think ;[5] Kipling might seem to be advocating the razing of barriers between human beings. But these lines are typical of his early not of his later, poetry ; and he limits his liberalism to "strong men", to men of action strong in limb and courage whom he characteristically admired. Both the Indian Border thief and the British Colonel's son are such men. These lines, uttered by the author, form the moral of this simple ballad. Kipling does not state or imply that the Indians and the British are equal as human beings. "Gunga Din" (1892 or earlier), a "barrack-room ballad", is wholly a monologue spoken by a British soldier. Through him Kipling presents a relationship between such a person and an Indian servant which appears worse than a feudal relationship between a European lord and a European serf. Probably, the servant matters to both Kipling and the soldier essentially because he is a "strong man", like the Border thief and the Colonel's son :

An' for all 'is dirty 'ide
'E was white, clear white, inside
When 'e went to tend the wounded under fire !

Kipling captures exactly the kind of idiom and attitudes an uneducated soldier would adopt. The idiom, which is public and colloquial, lends itself to reading aloud and recitation. The attitudes fit in with popular opinions. They are based on assumptions which are partly traditional and partly imperial : "white" has been traditionally a term of approval, and in imperial times it was associated with the Europeans to indicate (rather imprecisely) the colour of their skin and to stand for a conception of them as the sole bearers of civilization. But at the end Kipling permits the soldier to strike an attitude which, though rather conventional, would jolt the blimps :

Though I've belted you and flayed you,
By the livin' Gawd that made you,
You're a better man than I am, Gunga Din !

Kipling's more conventional attitudes and the popular vein in his poetry soon dominate his poetic practice. Not long after 1892 he began to use "*The Times* as a platform for major poems" (in Charles Carrington's phrase).[6] He steps into Tennyson's shoes as the spokesman and prophet of the Establishment. In 'A Song of the White Man' (1899), he welcomes the Boer War and is clearly imperialistic :

Now, this is the cup the White Men drink
When they go to right a wrong,

And that is the cup of the old world's hate—
Cruel and strained and strong,

We have drunk that cup—and a bitter, bitter cup—
And tossed the dregs away.

But well for the world when the White Men drink
To the dawn of the white Man's day !

The cup of life is a vague and hackneyed symbol, and the rhythm is mainly a kind of jingle. This kind of uplift—potent because it is indefinite—caters to the "average" mind and receives the "average" response, whether this is forthcoming from the reader of *The Times* or from the sections of the people who had done time in the Army or at least fallen for the jingoist mystique purveyed by the Harmsworth Press. When Kipling celebrates "the White Man's burden" he "reminds one of a man cheering to keep his courage up."[7] What makes A.E Rodway say this is no doubt the forced rhetoric of the versification. Unfortunately, such work is not sensitive enough for the latter-day reader to gauge whether Kipling, looks glumly ahead to the collapse of Empire because human arrangements necessarily fall apart or because the British ascendancy could already be seen to be in jeopardy. "Recessional" (1897) was meant to be a major poem about the Empire. It was written to mark Queen Victoria's Diamond Jubilee and was first published in *The Times*. It is a *locus classicus* for an examination of Kipling's maturest vision in poetry of imperial matters, including race relations.

> Far-called, our navies melt away ;
> On dune and headland sinks the fire :
>
> Lo, all our pomp of yesterday
> Is one with Nineveh and Tyre !
>
> Judge of the Nations, spare us yet,
> Lest we forget—lest we forget !
>
> If, drunk with sight of power, we loose
> Wild tongues that have not Thee in awe,
>
> Such boastings as the Gentiles use,
> Or lesser breeds without the Law—
>
> Lord God of Hosts, be with us yet,
> Lest we forget—lest we forget !

Kipling contemplates the British Empire in a historical light and foresees its inevitable dissolution. What is breath-taking is the sense we are palpably meant to get that it is extraordinarily noble for the poet of the master-race to concede this inevitability. He was intelligent enough to criticise extreme jingoism ; for example, in "The Flag of their Country" (*Stalky and Co.*) he suggests that there is considerable truth in the schoolboy's view of Mr. Raymond

Martin M.P. as "a Flopshus Cad, an Outrageous Stinker, a jelly-bellied Flag-flapper".[8] But the implications of "lesser breeds without the Law" are no less characteristic. The notorious phrase is obscure. It could refer to any, some or all, of the beings whom Kipling considers outside the pale of civilized order—the Indians in general, or "the Germans and especially the pan-German writers"[9] (as George Orwell thought), or the *Bandar-log* in *Jungle Book* or even the Wolves when they broke away from Akela and the Jungle Law to follow Shere Khan and their own unbridled appetites. The implication is that the British are the norm of a people within the Law, even that they are uniquely endowed with the qualities necessary to carry out best the tasks of imperialism. By the same token the "lesser breeds" are the people of the "undeveloped" countries—classed as "breed" because the spokesman of the dominant people cannot help thinking of the subject races in animal terms.

Rodway argues that "in Kipling's case no distinction between poetry and prose is necessary" and refers to works in both genres which have qualities in common.[10] But it seems to me that the remarkable works in each class—by which I mean both the works of rare skill *and* those that have become proverbial—make it plain that it was in his fiction that Kipling was keenly aware of social and psychological fact, whereas in his Indian poetry he was apt to surrender to the imperial wave.

NOTES

1. Joseph Chamberlain, "A Young Nation" (11 November, 1895): *Foreign and Colonial Speeches* (London : 1897), p. 89.
2. Chamberlain, "Splendid Isolation", op. cit., p. 93.
3. Cecil Rhodes, letter to W.T. Stead, quoted from C.E. Carrington, *The British Overseas* (London : 1950), p. 681.
4. All extracts from Kipling's poetry are from *Rudyard Kipling's verse Definitive Edition* (London : 1960 ed).
5. Jack Dunman, "Rudyard Kipling Re-estimated" : *Marxism Today* (1965), Vol. 9, No. 8, p. 243 ; M. Tarinayya, "East-West Encounter : Kipling" : *The Literary Criterion* (1966), Vol. 7, No. 3, p. 28.

6. Charles Carrington, *Rudyard Kipling : His Life and Work* (London : 1955), p. 258.
7. A.E. Rodway, "The Last Phase" : Boris Ford (ed.), *From D.ckens to Hardy* (London : 1958), p. 389.
8. Kipling, "The Flag of their Country" : *Stalky and Co.* (London : 1962 ed.), pp. 184-5.
9. George Orwell, "Rudyard Kipling" : Andrew Rutherford (ed.), *Kipling's Mind and Art* (London : 1965 ed.), p. 71.
10. A. E. Rodway, op. cit., p. 392.

CHAPTER 9

Race Relations in Shakespeare

In the old age black was not counted fair,
Or if it were, it bore not beauty's name ;
But now is black beauty's successive heir,
And beauty slander'd with a bastard shame ; ......

Sonnet 127

Because his society generally preferred a fair to a dark skin, Shakespeare feels it necessary to justify his love for the Dark Lady in his sonnets Skin colour is, objectively speaking, something neutral, but it has been given a value in conceptions of beauty. This kind of value is, probably, common to all ages and all communities : Ovid wrote,

> Nominibus mollire licet mala : fusca vocetur,
> Nigrior Illyrica cui pice sanguis erit : ......
>
> (With names you can soften shortcomings ; let her be called swarthy whose blood is blacker than Illyrian pitch ; ......)[1]

Aesthetic considerations of this kind have been confused with racial problems but I am virtually isolating racial problems for the purpose of this article. Racial problems first become important in Western literature in the age of Shakespeare, and this is historically logical. The Greeks and the Romans betrayed cultural prejudice, but not racial or colour prejudice,[2] though it is commonly thought that the Ancients considered the "barbarians" in the same way imperial-minded Europeans looked upon Asians and Africans [3] The age of Shakespeare was the age when the impact of the "voyages of discovery" of, say, Columbus, Vespucci and Vasco da Gama was conspicuous ; the age of Drake, Frobisher and Hakluyt ; the age when the trade in slaves, guns and sugar between Western Europe, West Africa and the West Indies was thriving ; and the age when the British East India Company was founded. Eldred Jones notes that "there were so many Negroes in London by 1601 that Elizabeth had cause to be 'discontented at the great number of Negars and blackmoors which are crept into the realm since the troubles between her Highness and the King of Spain', and for her to appoint a certain Caspar Van Zenden, merchant of Lubeck to transport them out of the country."[4] Thus Shakespeare is responding to the actual pressures of his age when he contemplates people alien to him racially.

His presentation of Shylock is a classic, and much-discussed, instance in this respect. Marlowe had surrendered to anti-semitism when he made Barabas in *The Jew of Malta* little more than a caricature of the conventional Jewish evil usurer. Anti-semitism was no less strong when Shakespeare wrote *The Merchant of Venice* : it was at this time that Roderigo Lopez, a Portuguese Jewish doctor, had been tried and publicly executed for an alleged attempt to assassinate the Queen. No doubt Shakespeare was aware of prejudices against the Jews : Shylock is time and again referred to as dog, wild beast and devil. But the question is whether Shakespeare himself followed the general contemporary view of the Jew. Here one can be guided by these pregnant words of Claude Lanzmann :

> a novel is a microcosm : if the only coward in it is a Jew, the only Jew a coward, an inclusive if not a universal relation is established between these two terms [5]

Lanzmann's paradigm applies to all forms of literature, not only to the novel, and to all the evils with which the Jews are traditionally associated, not only cowardice. It has an even wider relevance with which we are not concerned. In Shakespeare's play, the only inhumanly acquisitive person is a Jew, Shylock ; the only important Jew is an inhumanly acquisitive person. He is a contrast to Antonio who is Christian and unworldly, though a fellow trader. Thus, in a way, Shakespeare follows the traditionally preju iced view of the Jew and betrays 'the taint of racism". But this is far from all that there is to Shylock, as shown by this scene in a street in Venice :

Solanio. How now, Shylock ? What news among the merchants ?

Shylock. You knew, none so well, none so well as you, of my daughter's flight.

Salerio. That's certain ; I, for my part, knew the tailor that made the wings she flew withal.

Solanio. And Shylock, for his own part, knew the bird was flidge ; and then it is the complexion of them all to leave the dam.

Shylock. She is damn'd for it.

Salerio. That's certain, if the devil may be her judge.

Shylock. My own flesh and blood to rebel !

Solanio. Out upon it, old carrion ! Rebels it at these years ?

Shylock. I say my daughter is my flesh and my blood.

Salerio. There is more difference between thy flesh and hers than between jet and ivory; more between your bloods than there is between red wine and Rhenish. But tell us, do you hear whether Antonio have had any loss at sea or no ?

Shylock. There I have another bad match : a bankrupt, a prodigal, who dare scarce show his head on the Rialto ; a beggar, that was us'd to come so smug upon the mart. Let him look to his bond. He was wont to call me usurer; let him look to his bond. He was wont to lend money for a Christian courtesy; let him look to his bond.

Salerio. Why I am sure, if he forfeit, thou wilt not take his flesh. What's that good for ?

Shylock. To bait fish withal If it will feed nothing else, it will feed my revenge. He hath disgrac'd me and hind'red me half a million ; laugh'd at my losses, mock'd at my gains, scorned my nation, thwarted my bargains, cooled my friends, heated mine enemies. And what's his reason ? I am a Jew. Hath not a Jew eyes ? Hath not a Jew hands, organs, dimensions, senses, affections, passions, fed with the same food, hurt with the

> same weapons, subject to the same diseases, healed by the same means, warmed and cooled by the same winter and summer, as a Christian is ? If you prick us, do we not bleed ? If you tickle us, do we not laugh ? If you poison us, do we not die ? And if you wrong us, shall we not revenge ? If we are like you in the rest, we will resemble you in that. If a Jew wrong a Christian, what is his humility ? Revenge. If a Christian wrong a Jew, what should his sufference be by Christian example ? Why, revenge. The villainy you teach me I will execute; and it shall go hard but I will better the instruction.
>
> (Act III Scene 1.)

Shylock genuinely feels for his daughter and suffers because of her elopement. The prejudices against the Jews which he experiences in the course of his life in society, are real and are borne out by the behaviour of the Christians in the play. These prejudices, quite credibly, anger him and make him hard. The concluding lines suggest that revenge is an understandable human tendency, common to both Christians and Jews. Thus Shakespeare so presents Shylock that he has a convincing human quality which rises above the convention which stereotyped the Jews as monsters of greed.

When we turn to Shakespeare's treatment of relations between "white" people and "coloured" people, we must consider his presentation of the Indian boy in *A Midsummer-Night's Dream*, Aaron in *Titus Andronicus*, the Prince of Morocco in *The Merchant of Venice* and, above all, Othello. These are the only "coloured" people in Shakespeare when we use the term, "coloured", in its modern sense in the field of race relations.

In *A Midsummer-Night's Dream* (1595-6), Titania's changeling is "a lovely boy, stolen from an Indian king" (II. 1.). He is the cause of the quarrel between the King and the Queen of the fairies, but he never comes on stage. He is hardly interesting in his own right. But perhaps it is worth while attending to these lines from

Theseus' famous set piece on "The lunatic, the lover, and the poet";

> The lover, all as frantic,
> Sees Helen's beauty in a brow of Egypt.
> (V. 1.)

Helen, a Greek woman, is both fair and beautiful, whereas Shakespeare conceived the complexion of an Egyptian, even in *Antony and Cleopatra*, as both swarthy and ugly. Here Shakespeare is using the common notion that dark is to fair as ugliness is to beauty. His point is that a person in love will overlook the physical defects of his lady and that he will even be attracted to a dark complexion from which people in their right mind would recoil.

The authorship and date of *Titus Andronicus* are matters on which there is much doubt and disagreement among scholars, but the consensus is that it is an early play (c 1593) by Shakespeare. Aaron is, certainly, far more important to my theme than the Indian boy in *A Midsummer-Night's Dream*. Shakespeare calls him a Moor and he is constantly referred to as such by the other characters in the play. But Aaron refers to his hair as a "fleece" of "woolly" curly hair (II. 3.), while he describes his baby as "thick-lipped" (IV. 2.). These terms are particularly significant because that kind of hair and that kind of lips are a racial characteristic of negroes, not Moors In medieval times and as late as the 17th century, "white Moors" were known, but it was commonly believed that Moors were mostly black or very swarthy; indeed the word "Moor" was often used for "negro". These contemporary tendencies work with the imprecision of the conventional cursory Westerner's view of "coloured" people, an awareness of which made Joseph Conrad show Heyst telling Lena in *Victory*, "One Chinaman looks very much like another"[6]; obviously, realistically speaking, one "coloured" man is no more like another than one "white" man is like another when regarded in the same way. Shakespeare has succumbed to the conventional influences so that he unconsciously portrays Aaron, not in terms of a Moor, but in terms of a composite, figure of a "coloured" man.

The conventionality of Shakespeare's presentation of Aaron is prominent. *Titus Andronicus* is a melodrama and Aaron is its villain. Shakespeare is being quite conventional when he makes a black man the stage villain ; the black complexion was regarded in his time as symbolic of, and an explanation of, villainy. When Saturninus, Emperor of Rome, takes the Queen of the Goths, Tamora, as his Empress, Aaron declares his intentions to the audience :

> Then, Aaron, arm thy heart and fit thy thoughts
> To mount aloft with thy imperial mistress.
> And mount her pitch whom thou in triumph long
> Hast prisoner held, fett'red in amorous chains,
> And faster bound to Aaron's charming eyes
> Than is Promethus tied to Caucasus.
> Away with slavish weeds and servile thoughts !
> I will be bright and shine in pearl and gold,
> To wait upon this new-made emperess.
> To wait, said I ? To wanton with this queen,
> This goddess, this Semiramis, this nymph,
> This siren that will charm Rome's Saturnine,
> And see his shipwreck and his c mmonweal's.
>
> (II. 1.)

This is a conventional manifesto of a melodramatic villain. The metaphorical richness is one of the qualities of the poetry here that implies that Aaron is clever and that he enjoys his villainy, two traits which he shares with characters such as Marlowe's Barabas. His villainy is not sufficiently motivated. It is his villainy, rather than his liaison with Tamora, that is central to the play. He is quick-witted, heartless and meets with success : he contrives the murder of Bassianus and implicates Quintus and Martius in it ; he contrives the rape and mutilation of Lavinia. He finally over-reaches himself and goes unrepentantly to his death. His end enacts the simple moral that villainy does not pay.

Still, Aaron is not completely the stock Elizabethan Machiavel. He is "an irreligious Moor" (V. 3.) at a time when wicked Moors were supposed to be religious. He has one important redeeming quality, his affection for his child by Tamora. To the

Nurse, his child is "A joyless, dismal, black, and sorrowful issue !", but to Aaron the child is "a beauteous blossom" (IV. 2.). He sacrifices his own safety, his very life, for the sake of the child. Still, he does not become a fully human evil-doer like Iago.

In his treatment of Shylock in *The Merchant of Venice* (1596-7), we saw how Shakespeare's understanding and humanity were much in advance of average views of the Jew The same kind of advance is registered in his treatment of the "coloured" person in this play, the Prince of Morocco. The Prince is much less prominent in his play than Aaron was in his, but he is a fully human character. As one of Portia's suitors, he seems to me more interesting than Bassanio. He is not a mere outlandish figure as in a fair-ground pageant. The stage-directions in the Quarto describe him as "a tawny Moor all in white". The white costume suggests symbolically his inner worth, and an Elizabethan audience would easily gather this point as it was accustomed to this kind of simple symbolic presentation. Moreover, the fact that his complexion is "tawny" suggests that his character would not be as bad as those whose complexion is black. His opening words to Portia are :

> Mislike me not for my complexion,
> The shadowed livery of the burnish'd sun,
> To whom I am a neighbour, and near bred.
> (II. 1.)

He is self conscious about his colour and aware of prejudice against it, as Othello is going to be. But he is confident and proud and aware of his worth :

> I tell thee, lady, this aspect of mine
> Hath fear'd the valiant ; by my love, I swear
> The best-regarded virgins of our clime
> Have lov'd it too.
> (II. 1.)

Yet he concludes his opening speech thus :

> I would not change this hue,
> Except to steal your thoughts, my gentle queen.
> (II. 1.)

This is a compliment to Portia from a courtly personage, but underlying it is a sense of inferiority common among "coloured" races in their dealings with dominant "white" races. Portia assures him that were it not for the fact that her choice is "hedg'd" by the terms of her father's will,

> Yourself, renowned Prince, then stood as fair
> As any comer I have look'd on yet
> For my affection.
>
> (II. 1)

In the presence of the Prince of Morocco, she speaks with a polished hypocrisy which is a characteristic of sophisticated social intercourse as found at both Belmont and Venice. Portia adopts this manner to him partly because he is a man of high station and a man of means, though she belongs to a "ruling race" which, generally speaking, despises his. Indeed, she had openly displayed to her maid (and to the audience) her conventional racialist aversion to men of his "hue" before she met the Prince :

> If he have the condition of a saint and the complexion of a devil,
> I had rather he should shrive me than wive me.
>
> (I. 2.)

Thus, Shakespeare ironically shows up Portia's manners in this regard for what they are. Our impression of her kind of dissimulation is confirmed by her words when the Prince leaves after choosing the wrong casket :

> A gentle riddance. Draw the curtains, go.
> Let all of his complexion choose me so.
>
> (II. 7)

Shakespeare's handling of race relations develops interestingly. In *The Merchant of Venice*, he clearly departs from conventional Portrayals of "coloured" people and shows an awareness of the complexities of "coloured"—"white" relations. His development reaches its zenith in *Othello* (1604-5). The Prince of Morocco is, in a way, a sketch for the character of Othello : he is "coloured" but estimable ; he selects the golden casket because of his simple idealism. Love between members of "coloured" and "white" races was a minor theme in *Titus Andronicus* (the Aaron-Tamora relationship), but in *Othello* it is central and handled with incomparably greater skill and insight. Even in Shakespeare's portrayal of Othello, there is an element of conventionality. In the opening scene of the play, Roderigo slightingly and significantly refers to Othello's "thick-lips" ; though Shakespeare calls Othello a Moor and he is constantly referred to as such by the other characters, thick lips are (as I indicated earlier) a racial characteristic of negroes, not Moors. Thus, as in the case of Aaron, Shakespeare unconsciously portrays Othello, not in terms of a Moor, but in terms of a composite figure of a "coloured" man. But in other respects Shakespeare has advanced tremendously and Othello is presented with almost complete realism. This is indicated by the very fact that Othello is black but essentially different in character from Aaron ; he is not just "tawny" like the Prince of Morocco, but still a hero, and a hero of full tragic proportions, too. It is a "white" man, Iago, who is in line with Aaron in point of character. Shakespeare has realised that the value of a human being is not determined by the colour of his skin or his race.

Othello is different from the other members of Venetian society in the play in physique and cultural background. They respect him as a successful general whom they cannot do without ; at the same time, they look down on him as a social inferior because he is a "coloured" alien belonging to a race with little power. Even before he enters the stage, he is referred to slightingly : Iago calls him his "Moorship" and, as we have noticed, Roderigo mentions "the thick-lips" (I. 1.). Iago informs Brabantio that his daughter, Desdemona, has eloped with Othello:

> Even now, now, very now, an old black ram
> Is tupping your white ewe.
>
> (I. 1.)

Iago wants to excite Brabantio's revulsion from the match and he also reveals his own recoil in the process. The image from stock-breeding reduces the love of Othello and Desdemona to a coarse physical tie. It derives a part of its emotional force not only from the age difference between Othello and Desdemona but also from the racial difference. Iago and Roderigo are not the best representatives of Venetian society, but their attitudes to "coloured" people reflect, at least, average opinion. Brabantio is a respected counsellor of the Duke of Venice and we realize soon that his view of "coloured" people is no better. Prejudices against "coloured" people pervade Venetian society.

The tragedy of Othello's marriage to Desdemona is Shakespeare's central preoccupation in the play. The fact that the marriage is inter-racial, gives rise to problems which turn out to be important. Othello has to run away with Desdemona, a "white" Venetian, because of her father's opposition to their marriage. Brabantio's rage, when he discovers the elopement, reveals both the causes of his anger and of his opposition :

> O thou foul thief, where hast thou stow'd my daughter ?
> Damn'd as thou art, thou has enchanted her ;
> For I'll refer me to all things of sense,
> If she in chains of magic were not bound,
> Whether a maid so tender, fair, and happy,
> So opposite to marriage that she shunn'd,
> The wealthy curled darlings of our nation,
> Would ever have, to incur a general mock,
> Run from her guardage to the sooty bosom
> Of such a thing as thou—to fear, not to delight.
>
> (I. 2.)

Brabantio recoils from Othello's colour ; he feels acutely the general's social inferiority and the social stigma of a mixed marriage. Clearly, he is a conservative "white" Venetian. He puts his case to the Duke of Venice in these terms.

> She is abus'd, stol'n from me, and corrupted,
> By spells and medicines bought of mountebanks ;
> For nature so preposterously to err,
> Being not deficient, blind, or lame of sense,
> Sans witchcraft could not.
>
> (I. 3.)

He considers the relationship unnatural, refers to the supernatural and other peculiar means which were conventionally supposed to be open to 'coloured' people. Thus, racial elements in society, external to Othello, affect his status and the course and position of his relationship with Desdemona.

Before he enters the stage, Othello is spoken of with conventional contempt and prejudice, and he is the subject of Iago's machinations. This contrasts with and accents Othello's nobility of character which is expressed in his stance and speech as soon as he comes on stage. His colour not only emphasises his alienness in Venetian society. It serves to stress his nobility, for (as I have indicated) this was not a quality of character usually associated with a man of his race ; Shakespeare's audience would be, generally speaking, jolted. Still Othello is not an idealized black man; he has certain serious weaknesses, he is undone not so much by Iago's villainy as by these weaknesses of his. T. S. Eliot has observed Othello's "attitude of self-dramatization" and "*bovarysme*". F.R. Leavis has perceived "Othello's self-idealization, his promptness to jealousy and his blindness".[7] Othello is also too conscious of himself as a "coloured" alien in Venice. Iago's insinuations are persuasive partly because he bases them explicitly on his position as a "native" of Venice :

> I know our country disposition well :
> In Venice they do let God see the pranks
> They dare not show their husbands ; their best conscience
> Is not to leave't undone, but keep't unknown.
>
> (III. 3.)

Othello, as an alien, respects the words of "native", especially one whom he considers "honest". His kind of awareness of his race and colour makes him more vulnerable :

> Othello. I do not think but Desdemona's honest.
> Iago. Long live she so ! and long live you to think so !
> Othello. And yet, how nature erring from itself—
> Iago. Ay, there's the point : at—to be bold with you —
> Not to effect many proposed matches
> Of her own clime, complexion, and degree,
> Whereto we see in all things nature tends—

Foh ! one may smell in such a will most rank,
Foul disproportion, thoughts unnatural.
But pardon me—I do not in position
Distinctly speak of her ; though I may fear
Her will, recoiling to her better judgment,
May fall to match you with her country forms.
And happily repent.

(III. 3.)

Iago so plays upon the differences between Othello and Desdemona, in "clime, complexion, and degree", that he grows far more conscious of them than of the feelings that brought them together. This mentality, in turn, reveals the inadequacies of those feelings, leads to a distorted view of them and to a greater credulity. He is no longer masterful military captain :

. . . Haply for I am black.
And have not those soft parts of conversation.
That chamberers have, . . .

(III. 3.)

His loss of confidence is thus related to his colour and social position. The moment when Othello is almost convinced that his wife has been unfaithful, is revealing :

. . . Her name, that was as fresh
As Dian's visage, is now begrim'd and black
As mine own face.

III. 3.)

He links his wife's supposed deterioration with his own colour. When Emilia opens his eyes, he has already strangled Desdemona.

The problems that arise because Othello is a "coloured" alien in "white" Venetian society to which Desdemona belongs, play an important secondary role in Othello's tragedy. Leavis underestimates their importance when he says that Othello's colour is to be taken merely as "emphasizing the disparity of the match".[8] But G.M. Matthews topples ! over on the other side when he elaborates a thesis that "the recial contrast between Othello and his associates" is "the core of the play".[9]

What inferences can we draw from Shakespeare's plays as to his own views on race relations? The answers is, I think, none at all. To deduce Shakespeare's own opinions from the utterances of his characters is a dubious procedure. Words from *The Merchant of Venice* can be quoted to show that Shakespeare's view of the Jew is conventional; words can also be quoted from the same play to show that Shakespeare's view of the Jew is unconventional; Shylock can be played as villain and also as hero. Similarly, in *Othello*, it is Shakespeare's characters who enact the problems of a "coloured" alien in "white" society. Typically, Shakespeare not only treats his characters with an all-sided sympathy but also identifies himself with all of them. This is the way Shakespeare's genius works, and this does not seem to me a limitation on the value of his plays. We experience the problems of race relations as dramatized by him and are compelled to think afresh about this important aspect of the life of our time.

NOTES

1. Ovid, *Artis Amatoriae*, Book 2, 11.657-58. Translation — J.H. Mozley, *Ovid: The Art of Love and Other Poems* (London and Cambridge, Massachusetts: Heinemann and Harvard University Press, 1962 ed.), p. 111.
2. See M.I. Finley, "Race Prejudice in the Ancient World" : *The Listener*, 1 February 1968, pp. 146-7.
3. E.g., Arthur Ravenscroft writes sensibly but falls into this error in his "Editorial : Mr. Powell's Problem" : *The Journal of Commonwealth Literature* (July 1969), No. 7, p. vi.
4. Eldred Jones, *Othello's Countrymen : The African in English Renaissance Drama* (London : Oxford University Press, 1965), pp. 12-3.
5 Quoted from Simone de Beauvoir, *Force of Circumstance* (trans. Richard Howard, London : Penguin, 1968 ed.), p. 387.
6. Joseph Conrad, *Victory* (London: Methuen, 1954 ed.), p. 145.
7. T.S. Eliot, "Shakespeare and the Stoicism of Seneca" : *Selected Essays* (London: Faber and Faber 1963 ed.), pp. 129-31. F.R. Leavis, "Diabolic Intellect and the Noble Hero", *The common Pursuit* (London : Penguin, 1952 ed.), p. 145.

8. Leavis, op. cit., p. 142.
9. G.M. Matthews, "Othello and the Dignity of Man": Arnold Kettle (ed.), *Shakespeare in a Changing World* (London: Lawrence and Wishart, 1964), p. 124.

CHAPTER 10

Much Ado About Nothing Reconsidered

Much Ado About Nothing is the first of a group of three plays —the others are *As You Like It* and *Twelfth Night*—which were written just before the turn of the 16th century and are generally considered Shakespeare's greatest achievements in romantic comedy. Kenneth Muir regards these comedies as "the three masterpieces",[1] while M.C. Bradbrook writes :

> In the years between the death of Marlowe and Greene, and the arrival of Jonson and Chapman, the critical years between 1594 and 1598, Shakespeare had the stage virtually to himself. This was the period of his most rapid development. He grew from the experimenter of *Love's Labour Lost* and *Richard III* to the author of *Much Ado About Nothing*. It is an unequalled achievement. He was not only the greatest of the Elizabethan dramatists, but he did far more than any other man to create the drama and establish it.[2]

Miss Bradbrook's high opinion of *Much Ado* is shared by T.W. Craik : "there is nothing to prevent our complete enjoyment of the subtle comedy that Shakespeare is offering ; certainly there is no reason why we should find it in any sense a failure".[3] E.C. Pettet refers to *Much Ado* as "what has always been considered one of the greatest of Shakespeare's comedies".[4] But there is a contrary line of thinking particularly with regard to *Much Ado*. J.C. Maxwell regards it as "profoundly unsatisfactory",[5] while Patrick Swinden writes : "These two plays (*Much Ado About Nothing* and *All's Well that Ends Well*) are often considered the least satisfactory of Shakespeare's mature comedies, and I must say I share the prevailing dissatisfaction".[6] Thus, opinions about *Much Ado* tend to diverge sharply into the extremely favourable or the extremely unfavourable, and the determination of its true value calls for balanced discrimination.

Much Ado About Nothing, it seems to me, is a light comedy whose happy ending is assured. But Patrick Swinden is not far wrong when he claims that the play has "tragic potential".[7] Really, for a while the play moves close to Romantic Tragedy when Don John's villainy begins to work and Claudio spurns Hero, but the comedy reasserts itself. Claudio is clearly not another Romeo who would commit suicide for love. Although the main action belongs to Claudio and Hero and although Claudio's changing attitudes to Hero are the main source of the play's momentum, it is Benedick and Beatrice who emerge as the most interesting among the characters in the play and their comic wit circumscribes the area of the play. At a superficial level, both Benedick and Beatrice find their sophisticated humour adequate to deal with the fashionable world of the Court in which the play is set. For instance, when Beatrice chattering away with typical brightness provokes a mock invitation from Don Pedro, she uses her polished wit to refuse him without offending his dignity :

Don Pedro : Will you have me, Lady ?

Beatrice : No my Lord, unless I might have another for working-days, your Grace is too costly to wear every day : but I beseech your Grace pardon me, I was born to speak all mirth, and no matter.

(Act II, Scene i).

The play, however, obtrusively exploits wit too often for the sake of more entertainment, the resulting humour being far from purposive as, say, Falstaff's in *Henry IV*. This tends to make characters stooges of wit :

Leonato : You must not, sir, mistake my niece. There is a kind of merry war betwixt Signior Benedick and her, they never meet but there's a skirmish of wit between them.

Beatrice : Alas he gets nothing by that, in our last conflict, four of his five wits went halting off, and now is the whole man govern'd with one, so that if he have wit enough to keep himself warm, let him bear it for a difference between himself and his horse, for it is all the wealth that he hath left, to be known a reasonable creature. Who is his companion now ? he hath every month a new sworn brother.

Messenger : Is't possible.

Beatrice : Very easily possible, he wears his faith but as the fashion of his hat, it ever changes with the next block (I. i.)

Leonato's observation and the Messenger's question are openings for Beatrice's witty replies.

The popular comedy of the sub-plot reveals the sort of interest in Shakespeare that deepens to Falstaff, but here it, too, works in a non-serious way. It adds a refreshing, earthy dimension to the light entertainment the play provides, its language effectively exploiting contemporary common speech, its vigour, its knack of using profound concepts fantastically (for instance, Verges : Yea, or else it were pity but they should suffer salvation body and soul.—III. iii.). Much of this realistic homour is topical, as, say, the references to practices of Elizabethan Watchmen :

Dogberry : If you meet a thief, you may suspect him, by virtue of your office, to be no true man : and for such kind of men, the less you meddle or make with them, why the more is for your honesty.

Watch : If we know him to be a thief, shall we not lay hands on him ?

Dogberry : Truly by your office you may, but I think they that touch pitch will be defil'd : the most peaceable way for you, if you do take a thief, is, to let him show himself what he is, and steal out of your company. (III. iii.)

The sub plot also helps the play to tread only close upon Romantic Tragedy and no more. The Watchmen discover the conspiracy against Hero but their stupidity, plausibly enough, prevents them communicating their knowledge promptly. Yet, the very fact that the plot has been uncovered assures the audience that all the misunderstandings it has created are bound to be cleared up. And this sub plot hardly does anything more. It has hardly any serious function of significance in itself or in connection with the main plot. It is true that sometimes Dogberry and Verges seem to pour comic acid on the self-regarding qualities of the world of the court by their ridiculous display of the same :

> Conrade : Away, you are an ass, you are an ass.
>
> Dogberry : Dost thou not suspect my place ? dost thou not suspect my years ? O that he were here to write me down as ass ! but masters, remember that I am an ass, though it be not written down, yet forget not that I am an ass : No thou villain, thou art full of piety as shall be prov'd upon thee by good witness, I am a wise fellow, and which is more, an officer, and which is more, a householder, and which is more, as pretty a piece of flesh as any is in Messina, and one that knows the Law, go to, and a rich fellow enough, go to, and a fellow that hath had losses, and one that hath two gowns, and every thing handsome about him : bring him away : O that I had been writ down an ass ! (IV. ii.).

But, on the whole, their role is merely to purvey entertainment.

However, I do not wish to convey the impression that the whole play is an entirely light comedy, smoothly moving towards a happy conclusion. While the elements of Romantic Tragedy help rectify any false notion of easy, straight, entirely happy, smoothness of movement, the Benedick-Beatrice relationship reveals a theme somewhat serious and consistent, the theme of marriage. At first, both Beatrice and Benedick appear very sceptical of marriage :

Don Pedro : Well, as time shall try : in time the savage bull doth bear the yoke.

Benedick : The savage bull may, but if ever the sensible Benedick bear it, pluck off the bull's horns, and set them in my forehead, and let me be vilely painted, and in such great letters as they write, here is good horse to hire : let them signify under my sign, here you may see Benedick the married man. (I. i.)

Here we notice the recurring "bull" imagery that lends some continuity to the theme. Benedick seems to regard marriage as a concession to the animal in man, but he later grows to an acceptance of it, discarding his pose of scepticism (Beatrice's progress to this end will be seen to follow a slightly deeper course). In a characteristically Shakespearean way, prose is good enough to convey Benedick's surface tone of scepticism, but poetry is needed to communicate the final, more considered attitude to marriage found in his reply to Claudio :

Claudio : I think he thinks upon the savage bull :
Tush fear not man, we'll tip thy horns with gold,
And all Europa shall rejoice at thee,
As once Europa did at lusty Jove,
When he would play the noble beast in love.

Benedick : Bull Jove sir had an amiable low.
And some such strange bull leap'd your father's cow,
And got a calf in that same noble feat,
Much like to you, for you have just his bleast.
(V. iv.)

The "bull" imagery is used again ; in this instance, it helps to suggest the necessity of marriage for the continuity of life. This newfelt attitude goes hand in hand with, and gains conviction from, Benedick's final serious comment on the inadequacy of mere witty scepticism :

Don Pedro : How dost thou Benedick the married man ?

Benedick : I'll tell thee what Prince : a college of wit-crackers cannot flaut me out of my humour, dost thou think I care for a satire or an epigram ? no, if a man will be beaten with brains. a' shall wear nothing handsome about him : in brief, since I do purpose to marry, I will think nothing to any purpose that the world can say against it, and therefore never flout at me, for what I hav(aid against it : for man is a giddy thing, and t s is my conclusion : for thy part Claudio, I did ink to have beaten thee, but in that thou art li ; to be my kinsman, live unbruis'd and lo my cousin. (V. iv.)

And this theme of marriage is given an enhancing credibility by the humanity shown by Beatrice and Benedick, particularly when Hero is ' belied".

This theme is touched on, rather than carried out in a conti-nuous way, but its examination can be searching enough. It is Benedick and, more, Beatrice who are treated with most subtlety in the play. They provide much surface humour, and Benedick is at times only the licensed wit of the Elizabethan stage :

Benedick : That a woman conceived me, I thank her : that she brought me up, I likewise give her most humble thanks : but that I will have a recheat winded in my forehead, or hang my bugle in an invisible baldrick, all woman shall pardon me : because I will not do them the wrong to mistrust any, I will do myself the right to trust none : and the fine is (for the which I may go the finer), I will live a bachelor. (I. i.)

This speech is mere verbal jugglery. But as Benedick and Beatrice act as "professed tyrants" to each other's sex, there is at times an oversharpness in their language that is significant. For instance, Benedick's reply to Don Pedro's "I shall see thee ere I die, look pale with love" is too exaggeratedly vehement :

> With anger, with sickness, or with hunger, my Lord, not with love : prove that ever I lose more blood with love than I will get again with drinking, pick out mine eyes with a Ballad-maker's pen, and hang me up at the door of a brothel house for the sign of blind Cupid. (I. i.)

So too Beatrice :

> Benedick : Then is courtesy a turn-coat, but it is certain I am loved of all Ladies, only you excepted : and I would I could find in my heart that I had not a hard heart, for truly I love none.
>
> Beatrice : A dear happiness to women, they would else have been troubled with a pernicious suitor : I thank God and my cold blood, I am of your humour for that, I had rather hear my dog bark at a crow, than a man swear he loves me. (I. i.)

Later, Beatrice unerringly pierces Benedick at his weakest point :

> Why he is the Prince's jester, a very dull fool, only his gift is, in devising impossible slanders, none but libertines delight in him, and the commendations is not in his wit, but in his villainly, for he both pleases men and angers them, and then they laugh at him, and beat him : I am sure he is in the Fleet, I would he had boarded me. (II. i.)

It is the charge that he is an official jester rather than that he is a poor jester that offends Benedick. This is so telling because he, like Beatrice, sometimes does show an awareness of his humorous front that saves him from being ridiculous :

> Benedick : O she misus'd me past the endurance of a block : an oake but with one green leaf on it, would have answered her : my very visor began to assume life, and scold with her : she told me, not thinking I had been myself, that I was the Prince's jester, that I was duller than a great thaw, huddling jest upon jest, with such impossible conveyance upon me, that I stood like a man at a mark, with a whole army shooting at me : . . . (II. i.)

The extra sharpness in the language of Benedick and Beatrice suggests that their witty scepticism is a semi-conscious pose covering up a deeper emotional condition. This is more so in the case of Beatrice whose emotional state is finely, though unknowingly, defined by Hero :

> But Nature never fram'd a woman's heart,
> Of prouder stuff than that of Beatrice :
> Disdain and Scorn ride sparkling in her eyes,
> Misprising what they look on, and her wit
> Values itself so highly, that to her
> All matter else seems weak : she cannot love,
> Nor take no shape nor project of affection,
> She is so self endeared.
>
> (III. i)

Thus, in her diatribes against the male Beatrice seems to be using her wit to rationalise a dissatisfaction springing from an inability to enter into a relationship with a man. That the dissatisfaction is connected with Benedick is suggested, for one, by the curiously serious words Beatrice utters in the midst of a comic scene :

> Done Pedro : Come Lady, come, you have lost the heart of Signior Benedick.
>
> Beatrice : Indeed my Lord, he lent it me awhile, and I gave him use for it, a double heart for his single one, marry once before he won it of me, with false dice, therefore your Grace may well say I have lost it. (II. i.)

Beatrice and Benedick seem to have established a relationship in the past and Benedick seems to have broken it. Their persisting mutual concern beneath the surface antagonism is hinted at from the beginning. It is Beatrice who introduces Benedick to the play by inquiring after him :

> Beatrice : I pray you, is Signior Mountanto return'd from the wars or no ? (I i.)

Benedick would rail against her :

> . . . she speaks poniards, and every word stabs : if her breath were as terrible as her terminations, there were no living near

> her, she would infect to the north star : I would not marry her, though she were endowed with all that Adam had left him before he transgress'd she would have made Hercules have turn'd spit, yea, and have cleft his club to make the fire too ; come, talk not of her, you shall find her the infernal Ate in good apparel, I would to God some scholar would conjure her, for certainly, while she is here, a man may live as quiet in hell, as in a sanctuary, and people sin upon purpose, because they would go thither, so indeed all disquiet, horror, and perturbation follows her. (II. i.)

But his interest in her is subtly suggested by the idea contained in "I would not marry her", an idea not yet given him by any other person. Therefore, the gulling scenes form only the machinery which enables them to discard their defensive poses when the playwright has no use for them. Still, both have a psychologically explicable, human depth of character, though Benedick less so as he is closer to the licensed stage wit. At the wedding scene, of those who belong to the society of "fashion", only they show humanity and understanding. Beatrice's fidelity and spontaneity not seen to great advantage in the comic world, bursts out :

> O on my soul my cousin is belied. (IV. i.)

Benedick hesitates but, spurred by love, agrees to "Kill Cloudio" (IV. i.)

Against Benedick and Beatrice are placed Don Pedro, Claudio and Leonato. Don Pedro is not scrutinised closely, although some criticism is implied in that he supports Claudio in the darker scenes. Claudio is viewed more critically. Superficially, Claudio is the romantic lover of the Elizabethan stage ; he speaks thus to Benedick in praise of Hero :

> In mine eyes, she is the sweetest Lady that ever I look'd on. (I. i.)

But really he is callously self-regarding ; he is concerned to find out whether Hero is Leonato's heir before acquiescing in Don Pedro's proposal to woo Hero on his behalf ; he talks thus in the eavesdropping scene where Don Pedro, Leonato and Claudio gull Benedick :

> Stalk on, stalk on, the fowl sits.
> .. ..
> Bait the hook well.
> ....
> He hath ta'en th' infection. (II. iii.)

The heartlessness, revealed by the nastiness of his witty language here, culminates in his cruel spurning of Hero :

> Give not this rotten orange to your friend
> She's but the sign and semblance of her honour :
> Behold how like a maid she blushes here !
> O what authority and show of truth
> Can cunning sin cover itself withal !
> Comes not that blood, as modest evidence,
> To witness simple virtue ? would you not swear
> All you that see her, that she were a maid,
> By these exterior shows ? But she is none :
> She knows the heat of a luxurious bed :
> Her blush is guiltiness, not modesty.
> (IV. i.)

Clearly, he is less romantic than Benedick and Beatrice as brought out, for one, by their attitudes to him and Hero after the spurning.

Yet all these glimpses of serious meaning in *Much Ado* do not go to form a consistently significant whole. Claudio is criticised, but the language fails in consistency as regards the criticism made. In the last scene, he agrees to marry a person who he thinks is Hero's cousin "were she an Ethiope", but this is presented not so much as final proof of his innate shallowness but as a necessary part of the action. The delaying of the inevitable happy climax to extract some not very deep suspense and the balancing of structural elements, as in the two main eavesdropping scenes, only reveals a certain cleverness on the part of the dramatist. The plot is obtrusively manipulative. Its main technique is to exploit conventions such as errors, overhearings, but, worked out through weak prose and weak poetry, these appear mechanical and make the characters seem too often mere puppets. This applies even to the bringing together of Benedick and Beatrice and it seems an arbitrary stage tie-up rather than some-thing psychologically real :

> This can be no trick, the conference was sadly borne. They have the truth of this from Hero, they seem to pity the Lady : it seems her affections have their full bent : love me ? why it must be requited : I hear how I am censur'd, they say I will bear myself proudly, if I perceive the love come from her : they say too, that she will rather die than give any sign of affection : I did never think to marry, I must not seem proud, happy are they that hear their detractions, and can put them to mending : they say the Lady is fair, 'tis a truth, I can bear them witness : and virtuous, 'tis so, I cannot reprove it, and wise, but for loving me, by my troth it is no addition to her wit, nor no great argument of her folly, for I will be horribly in love with her. I may chance have some odd quirks and remnants of wit broken on me, because I have railed so long against marriage : but doth not the appetite alter ? a man loves the meat in his youth, that he cannot endure in his age. Shall quips and sentences, and these paper bullets of the brain awe a man from the career of his humour ? No, the world must be peopled. When I said I would die a bachelor, I did not think I should live till I were married, here comes Beatrice : by this day, she's a fair Lady, I do spy some marks of love in her. (II. i.)

This is Benedick speaking, after the eavesdropping device has been used on him. The patterned prose, not following the run of common speech, takes the form of a sort of debate (with the enumeration of points—"... they seem ... they say ... they say too ... they say. . .", with questions and answers) and conveys the impression of an artificial cold logicality rather than of the warm inward movements of a heart leading towards a decided change of attitude. The convention remains merely mechanical. So, too, in the case of Beatrice :

What fire is in mine ears ? can this be true ?
Stand I condemn'd for pride and scorn so much ?
Contempt, farewell, and maiden pride, adieu,
No glory lives behind the back of such.
And Benedick, love on I will requite thee,
Taming my wild heart to thy loving hand :
I thou dost love, my kindness shall incite thee
To blind our loves up in a holy band.
For others say thou dost deserve, and I
Believe it better than reportingly. (III. i.)

Here poetry is used with the same result. This speech of Beatrices, in the first place, does not seem in character. She can hardly be so artless as this, nor had she revealed an uncontrollably "wild heart". It is in keeping with the courtly code that Beatrice seems to want to fall openly in love with Benedick as some kind of reciprocal duty, but the speech is too brief, the verse too stilted, to convincingly communicate warm inward movements of the heart. Conventions to be dramatically effective must be brought to life as, say, in *The Winter's Tale* ;

Leontes (Aside) : Too hot, too hot !
To mingle friendship far is mingling bloods.
I have tremor cordis on me; my heart dances,
But not for joy, not joy. This entertainment
May a free face put on ; drive a liberty
From heartiness, from bounty, fertile bosom,
And well become the agent. 'T may, I grant ;
But to be paddling palms and pinching fingers,
As now they are, and making practis'd smiles
As in a looking-glass ; and then to sigh, as 'twere
The mort o'th' deer. O, that is entertainment
My bosom likes not, nor my brows !
(I. ii.)

Leontes' sudden obsessive jealousy is made plausible by the power of the poetry here, though not prepared for ealier.

The general lightness of *Much Ado* is now very clear, but from this I am unable to proceed to James Smith's assumption of a special world of the play.[8] The staging would make it obvious that the play is set in the fashionable world of the Court, yet this too often forms a lifeless backdrop as it were. The word "fashion" recurs, but not in such a way as to help recreate a society that is thematically significant. It is only at stray points (for instance, in that eavesdropping scene when Claudio's language is charged with that repelling nastiness capable of breaking through convention) that the words are strong enough to give an inkling of the kind of culpably frivolous society Smith imagines existing as a whole in the play.[9] Assuming the creation of such a society, Smith can only oversimply treat Benedick's and Beatrice's cynicism as a conscious pose to protect themselves from others of the oppposite sex so as to keep themselves free for each other.[10] It has been my contention that theirs were semi-conscious, rather than conscious, poses adopted to cover up their real emotional condition.

The language of the play reaches a high point in the poetry of Leonato's speeches after the "tragedy". It is the clearest sign in the play of Shakespear's future greatness.

> I pray thee cese thy counsel,
> Which falls into mine ears as profitless,
> As water in a sieve : give me not counsel,
> Nor let no comforter delight mine ear,
> But such a one whose wrongs do suit with mine.
> Bring me a father that so lov'd his child,
> Whose joy of her is overwhelm'd like mine,
> And bid him speak of patience,
> ....
> No, no, 'tis all men's office, to speak patience
> To those that wring under the load of sorrow
> But no man's virtue nor sufficiency
> To be so moral, when he shall endure
> The like himself : therefore give me no counsel,
> My griefs cry louder than advertisement. (V. i.)

The over moral over insistence in Leonato's refusal of consolation suggests that he is keeping up the role of a prostrate father with self-pitying and self-regarding tendencies rather than expressing genuine heart felt grief over Hero's plight. Showing already a capacity to control lines as they run off the metre, Shakespeare communicates a breathlessness that indicates a concern in Leonato to convince others and himself of the genuineness of his emotion. This essentially poetic and essentially dramatic method of revealing character through speech whose full import is unknown to the speaker points to Shakespeare's mature works. In Othello's famous last speech basically the same thing is done, through more subtly and economically :

> No more of that. I pray you, in your letters,
> When you shall these unlucky deeds relate,
> Speak of me as I am ; nothing extenuate,
> Not set down aught in malice. Then must you speak
> Of one that lov'd not wisely, but too well ;
> Of one not easily jealous, but being wrought,
> Perplexed in the extreme ; of one whose hand,
> Like the base Indian, threw a pearl away
> Richer than all his tribe ; of one whose subdu'd eyes,
> Albeit unused to the melting mood,
> Drops tears as fast as the Arabian trees
> Their med'cinable gum......
>
> (V. ii.)

Without recourse to relatively easy over insistence, Shakespeare is able to convey superbly a poignant sense of heightened tragedy as Othello tries to deceive himself as regards his fatal jealousy.

There is hardly any other poetry of the quality of Leonato's later speeches in *Much Ado*. I have already pointed out that the play does not form a significantly satisfactory whole. Its conventions generally remain unrealised and its characters seem to often mere puppets. Both its main plot and sub-plot largely provide only entertainment, and a play at this level or comedy has to close with happy marriages. The manipulative plot mech anism, by its very manipulativeness, also assures us of the happy pairing off of Claudio and Hero, Benedick and Beatrice. Moreover, Don John does not embody any real evil capable of upsetting the play's comic equilibrium. He is the conventional "plain-dealing villain", a mere puppet of evil, who is made to appear infrequently mainly to work out that element of Romantic Tragedy. Shakespeare takes care to provide a motive for Don John's villainy :

Borachio : Being entertain'd for a perfumer, as I was smoking a musty room, comes me the Prince and Claudio, hand in hand in sad conference : I whipt me behind the arras, there heard it agreed upon, that the Prince should woo Hero for himself, and having obtain'd her, give her to Count Claudio.

John : Come, come, let us thither, this may prove food to my displeasure, that young start-up hath all the glory of my overthrow : if I can cross him any way, I bless myself every way : you are both sure, and will assist me.

Conrade : To the death my Lord.

(I. iii,)

Yet his is a mechanical role, lacking significance :

Messenger : My Lord, your brother John is taken in flight,
And brought with armed men back to Messina.

Benedick : Think not on him till tomorrow, I'll devise three brave punishments for him : strike up pipers.

Dance. (V. iv.)

Benedick refuses to think Don John and problems worth consideration, and decides to carry on with the dance, thus closing the play on this light note in keeping with its general level of entertainment. Yet Shakespeare's talent does manage to achieve something more despite this. I have indicated serious elements in the play. Leonato's later poetry and the racy vernacular comic prose are clearly promising excellencies.

Much Ado is not a "masterpiece". Nor is it "profoundly unsatisfactory". It seems to me to have a mixed value and is, from one aspect, a transitional work from Shakespeare's early comedies to that extraordinary period in the opening years of the 17th century which gave us *Twelfth Night* and *As You Like It* as well as *Julius Caesar* and *Hamlet*.

NOTES

1. Kenneth Muir (ed.), *Shakespeare the Comedies* (New Jersey : Prentice-Hall, 1965), p. 1.
2. M.C. Bradbrook, *Shakespeare and Elizabethan Poetry* (London: Chatto and Windus, 1951), p. 83.
3. T.W. Craik, 'Much Ado About Nothing' : *Scrutiny*, Vol. 19, No. 4, p. 316.
4. E.C. Pettet, *Shakespeare and the Romance Tradition* (London : Methuen, 1970 ed.) p. 132.
5. J.C. Maxwell, 'Shakespeare : The Middle Plays' : Boris Ford (ed.), *The Age of Shakespeare* (London : Penguin, 1955), p. 203.
6. Patrick Swinden, *An Introduction to Shakespeare's Comedies* (London : Macmillan, 1973) p. 88.
7. Patrick Swinden, op. cit., p. 100.
8. James Smith, 'Much Ado About Nothing' : *Scrutiny*, Vol. 13, No. 4, p. 245.
9. James Smith, op. cit., pp. 245, 251.
10. James Smith, op. cit. p. 250.

CHAPTER 11

The Tempest

A NOTE ON ITS SIGNIFICANCE FOR 'DEVELOPING' COUNTRIES

It was in the period of Elizabeth I that the 'developing' world was first brought prominently to the notice of the British consciousness—for this was the age when the impact of the 'voyages of discovery' of Columbus, Vespucci, Vasco da Gama and others was conspicuous; this was the age of Drake, Frobisher and Hakluyt; the age when the trade in slaves, guns and sugar between Western Europe, West Africa and the West Indies was thriving, the age when the British East India Company was founded. These pressures generated an exoticism partly because few Englishmen at that time knew, or cared, much about the actualities. But Shakespeare was not indifferent, though he shared something of the contemporary ignorance.

The clash of European civilization and primitive culture, which occurred in 'undeveloped' environments as a consequence of European activity overseas, is Shakespeare's theme in *The Tempest.* Prospero is the ruler of Caliban's 'undeveloped' island. He is educated and this fact indicates an advancement brought about by civilization. But Shakespeare also shows an evil aspect to it: Sebastian and Antonio indulge in political trickery. These courtiers themselves are differentiated: the weaker, less guilty Sebastian needs the more ruthless Antonio to egg him on. Thus civilization is presented in a carefully qualified way. The Island itself is enchanting and pure; yet the life on it is extremely primitive as Caliban's role shows. Thus Shakespeare is presenting a place more real than a simple lotus-eating isle. He goes even further: these are the plans of the garrulous old courtier, Gonzalo, if he had the "plantation of the isle":

I' th' commonwealth I would by contraries
Execute all things; for no kind of traffic
Would I admit; no name of magistrate;
Letters should not be known; riches, poverty,
And use of service, none; contract, succession,
Bourn, bound of land, tilth, vineyard, none;
No use of metal, corn, or wine, or oil;
No occupation; all men idle, all;
And women too, but innocent and pure;
No sovereignty. . . (Act II sc. I.)

Shakespeare enhances the reality of the island by showing us how, in this instance, it's ideal atmosphere could be given an absurd twist by a civilized person. Gonzalo's is a dream of an ideal of idleness and simplicity; virtually, of anarchism. Thus, there is no simple contrast, or simple interaction, between the civilized and the primitive.

This kind of complex vision lies behind Shakespeare's portrayal of Prospero and Caliban, his main characters and the chief representatives of the two stages of existence. Prospero is an equivalent in romance of one type of district officer. I have suggested that his education has a value, but it does not make him a good ruler. Magic gives him an arbitrary authority, and he often exercises it oppressively:

Caliban. As wicked dew as e'er my mother brush'd
With raven's feather from, unwholesome fen
Drop on you both! A south-west blow on ye
And blister you all o'er!

Prospero. For this, be sure, to-night thou shalt have cramps,
Side-stitches that shall pen thy breath up: urchins
Shall, for that vast of night that they may work,
All exercise on thee; thou shalt be pinch'd
As thick as honeycomb, each pinch more stinging
Than bees that made 'em. (I.2.)

The play is most real at moments such as this one when the civilized and the primitive clash openly. Both Prospero and Caliban resort to a peculiarly venomous language. But whereas Caliban's speech is in the vein of impotent folk imprecation, Prospero's language is educated and linked to precise harsh punishments that would be inflicted on Caliban. Thus by establishing a certain similarity, as well as by differentiating, between their speech. Shakespeare 'places' both. Prospero's attitude to Ariel goes with that towards Caliban: he reacts thus when the spirit asks to be set free:

> If thou more murmur'st I will rend an oak
> And peg thee in his knotty entrails, till
> Thou hast howl'd away twelve winters. (I 2)

As Ariel never opposes his master even verbally, Prospero's severity seems unwarrante . Thus, through Prospero's treatment of Caliban and Ariel, Shakespeare shows how authority can become a rather inhuman weapon of repression in civilized hands.

He depicts Caliban with even greater insight and complexity than Prospero. Caliban is partly an embodiment of primitive nature itself; there is truth when Prospero calls him "Thou earth, thou!" He is also the typical aboriginal inhabitant whose impulses have not been directed by civilization. He instigates Trinculo and Stephano to supplant Prospero and has grave misgivings.

> . . . We shall lose our time,
> And all be turn'd to barnacles, or to apes
> With foreheads villainous low. (IV. 1.)

Caliban's fears are absurdly superstitious; it is a jester and a drunken butler whom he sees as fit alternative rulers to Prospero; the change in his position he wants to effect is from Prospero's slave to their "foot licker". Thus, Shakespeare ironically reveals the primitiveness of a mind such as Caliban's and suggests that primitive human beings would remain in subjection whatever the changes of rule because they can do no better. Still, there are potentialities for development in Caliban. A part of his nature suggests destructive possibilities: he wishes to get rid of the civilized rule of Prospero and the murder of his master seems to him an unexceptionable method. He reveals an even worse tendency in his words to Prospero about his kind of desire to "violate" Miranda:

> O ho, O, ho! Would't had been done.
> Thou didst prevent me; I had peopl'd else
> This isle with Calibans. (I. 2)

Caliban seems to revel idiot-like in unbridled natural power and gloat over the horrible. Thus, the positive side of Caliban can become definitely ugly, not merely destructive. But he also has potentialities which show that he could benefit by contact with civilization. He can pick up civilized speech from Prospero. He responds to the atmosphere of the island:

> ...The isle is full of noises,
> Sounds, and sweet airs; that give delight and hurt not.
> Sometimes a thousand twangling instruments
> Will hum about mine ears; and sometimes voices.
> That, if I then had wak'd after long sleep,
> Will make me sleep again: and then, in dreaming,
> The clouds methought would open and show riches
> Ready to drop upon me, that, when I wak'd.
> I cried to dream again. (III. 2.)

Shakespeare employs Caliban's words to help build the ideal spell-bound atmosphere of the island and, at the same time, to reveal an aspect of his character. Caliban uses mellow tones exceptional for him, a sensuous auditory image, a climactic visual image in biblical language suggesting a miracle; and the pausing run of poetry confirms our sense of his pathetic bewildered sensitivity to "sounds and sweet airs that give delight". His dreaming enhances our sense of his 'humanness' as this is a peculiarly human quality.

In *The Tempest*, then, Shakespeare presents the civilized and the primitive as having a mixed value. More than a century later, in *Robinson Crusoe*, Defoe presented the same theme as *The Tempest.* His attitudes emerge clearly in his rendering of Crusoe's relationship with Man Friday. He implicitly endorses Crusoe's attitudes and actions. He assumes that the 'benighted savage' must be civilized in a domineering way and this meant that he must be made European Shakespeare's point of view appears astonishingly perceptive and balanced, and far ahead of his time.

CHAPTER 12

Conrad as a Modernist Writer:

THE SECRET AGENT

> The fact is you want more scepticism at the very foundation of your work. Scepticism, the tonic of minds, the tonic of life, the agent of truth,— the way of art and salvation.
>
> Contrad, Letter to John Galsworthy, 11 November 1901.

Joseph Contrad's works are usually taken together with 20th century literature so that we are inclined to forget that more than half his life was spent in the 19th century and that it was in the 19th century that he began his career as a writer. *Almayer's Folly*, his first fictional effort, was published in 1895, and it was followed by An *Outcast of the Islands* in 1896. Both these Malayan novels are prentice work; they reveal faint signs of Conrad's later greatness but are written very much in the vein of the conventional exotic fiction of the late 19th century. When *The Nigger af the 'Narcissus'* appeared in 1897, Conrad unmistakably showed for the first time that his talent was extraordinary, yet he is still recognisably a 19th century writer. He is very much a 19th century realist and he celebrates the traditional values of the Merchant Service such as courage, discipline, loyalty, endurance and collaborative endeavour. It is true that he suggests the limitations of these values: while these values enable the European seamen to deal with grave but straightforward and not unfamiliar problems such as those caused by the storm, these values do not equip *the ordinary sailors* to cope with serious, unfamiliar, subtle problems such as those posed by Donkin and, above all, by James Wait. Still Conrad's emphasis is on the strength of these values rather than on their frailties : Old Singleton and *the officers* are always equal to the problems posed by nature as well as by human beings such as Donkin and Wait. Conrad, however, becomes modernistic as he develops, and this tendency first declares itself in his technique. His objectivity becomes more scrupulous, his use of material more strictly economical and his novelistic structure organic yet independent of plot. These aspects of technique are triumphantly employed in *Lord Jim*, published in 1900, while his novelistic vision is still of a piece with *The Nigger of the 'Narcissus'*. It is in *Nostromo*, issued in 1904, that not only Conrad's technique but his artistic vision becomes modernistic: he becomes sceptical of the strength validity of all moral values. The values of all his characters, ranging from public prestige esteemed by Nostromo to scepticism itself upheld by Decoud, are tested against the silver and emerge as more or less qualified. Yet a trace of 19th century faith remains in Contrad's vision even in his greatest work. It is true that Giorgio Viola, "the idealist of the old humanitarian revolutions,"[1] is an old man and an immigrant who cannot affect or take part in the affairs of Costaguana; Captain Mitchell, who retains the values of the Merchant Service, and Don Pepe, who is the loyal retired military man, are rather dense and actively support the "material interests". But the values of Giorgio Viola, Captain Mitchell and Don Pape are able to withstand the corruption usually wrought by the silver. When Conrad writes *The Secret Agent* (1907), his talent develops further and is fully modernistic in both technique and artistic vision. It is mainly his vision that I wish to examine here.

In a letter to R.B. Cunninghame Graham of 7th October 1907, Conrad wrote of *The Secret Agent*: "It had some importance for me as a new departure in *genre* and is a sustained effort in ironical treatment of a melodramatic subject."[2] Both Conrad's viewpoint and fictional mode are ironic. It is true that in *Heart of Darkness* (1902) he had employed an ironic method through a narrator, Marlow,[3] but the irony of *The Secret Agent* is of a different quality and is deployed without a narrator. The novel is thus, for Conrad, "a new departure in genre". Its "subject" is usually the stuff of melodrama—the life of a double agent, embassy plotting, a bomb blast, accidental death, suicide and underground revolutionists. But Conrad's controlling interests are not those of a writer of melodrama.

F.R. Levis suggests that the central theme of the novel is "insulation."[4] Certainly, "insulation" describes accurately the relationship of Adolf Verloc and Winnie, both before and after marriage. But it seems to me that the central and developing theme is about betrayal. The basic tendencies of Mr. Verloc's character are towards order, opulence, indolence and respectable domestication but, in ironic contrast, his home is lower middle class and squalid, his associates revolutionists, his profession that of a double agent (he is both a spy for the Russian Embassy and a police informer). Thus, Verloc has betrayed his true nature by his chosen way of life. His innate bias towards secretiveness and his profession induce him to keep Winnie in the dark about his way of life, and he thus betrays his wife. Yet Verloc gains by contrast with his associates, the anarchists, Karl Yundt, Comrade Ossipon, Michaelis and the Professor. Verloc is like one of us whereas the anarchists seem a breed apart; Chief Inspector Heat rightly recognises, with a shock of horror, the alienness of the rebels when he accidentally runs into the Professor in the street. Verloc's appearance is untidy and flabby: "he had an air of having wallowed, fully dressed, all day on an unmade bed:"[5] the first remark made by Mr. Vladimir, the First Secretary of the embassy of Czarist Russia, when he sees Verloc, is "He's fat—the animal" (p. 19). His appearance reflects Conrad's moral disapproval but he is much less repelling than the anarchists. He even has an element of worthiness and an appeal which the anarchists lack. He is a man more sinned against than sinning. He ruins not only his family but himself. He brings about ruin because he is weak in a human way rather than because he is actively evil.

Conrad seems to have thought that Winnie is a more important character than Verloc. He seems to have thought she is the heroine of the novel in the conventional sense, that the story is her story, that she is heroic, that she wins and deserves the wholehearted sympathy of the reader.[6] Christopher Cooper virtually subscribes to these views.[7] Can be agree ? Winnie's life before she accepted Mr. Verloc's offer of marriage is relevant to our assessment of her. Her mother remembers:

> There had been a steady poung fellow, only son of a butcher in the next street, helping his father in business, with whom Winnie had been walking out with obvious gusto. He was

> dependent on his father, it is true; but the business was good, and his prospects excellent. He took her girl to the theatre on several evenings. Then just as she began to dread to hear of their engagement (for what could she have done with that big house alone, with Stevie on her hands), that romance came to an abrupt end, and Winnie went about looking very dull. (p. 40)

The son of the butcher did not have the means to provide for Stevie, Winnie's half-witted younger brother, and her mother, whereas Mr. Verloc had, and this fact alone makes Winnie decide in favour of Verloc, though the butcher's son was closer to her in age, was more attractive and had won her affection. Winnie has the capacity to love and she betrays her own nature when she contracts a marriage of convenience with Verloc of her own free will. After marriage, her love as such was only for Stevie and this is a betrayal of her husband. The intensity of her feelings for the boy had its origins in her childhood—"As a little girl she had often faced with blazing eyes the irascible licensed victualler (their father) in defence of her brother" (p. 38)—and remains undiminished. It is true that her love for Stevie is partly selfless. The boy needed a home and protection; he could not tend for himself. He does not appeal to her for help, but she looks after him of her own accord and gains nothing materially thereby. Yet, emotionally, Winnie does gain from Stevie. He provides her with an object for affection, both before and after marriage. The feelings which he evokes in Winnie, are a substitute for her want of love for her husband and the absence of children. These feelings introduce a savour into the otherwise tasteless life of a double agent's wife. Thus Winnie's devotion to Stevie has its self-aggrandizing aspect. It is not heroic self-abnegation. I cannot but disagree with Christopher Cooper: "Winnie Verloc is throughout motivated by a concern for her idiot brother which in its quality amounts to that nobility which stems from a desire to make life easier for others and operates to the complete exclusion of self-interest."[8] I deny that Winnie achieves "nobility". Her "self-interest" is unconscious, but it is there.

Verloc assumes that he is loved by Winnie for his own sake, and the reader sympathises with him in his error. Winnie throughout conceals from him the true state of her heart. Moreover, while betraying Verloc in this important respect, she assumes that Verloc loves her for her own sake and expects this kind of love as a matter of right:

> In the early days, made sceptical by the trials of friendless life, she (Winnie's mother) used sometimes to ask anxiously: "You don't think, my dear, that Mr. Verloc is getting tired of seeing Stevie about ?" To this Winnie replied habitually by a slight toss of her head. Once, however, she retorted with a rather grim pertness: "He'll have to get tired of me first". (p. 40)

Winnie's mind was very limited: a "distant and uninquiring acceptance of facts was her force and safeguard in life". (p. 153) With such a mind, she was extremely fortunate in engaging the affections of the butcher's son and she must indeed be thankful for having secured even Mr. Verloc as her husband. The relationship of Verloc and Winnie is carefully defined by Conrad:

> Their accord was perfect, but it was not precise. It was a tacit accord, congenial to Mrs. Verloc's incuriosity and to Mr. Verloc's habits of mind, which were indolent and secret. They refrained from going to the bottom of facts and motives. (p. 245)

Both Verloc and Winnie are equally responsible for what their marital relationship is. It is superficial and vague, the husband and wife are insulated from each other. Yet it is precisely because of its superficiality and vagueness and the insulation that the marriage achieves a kind of success. Both have confidence in each other's fidelity and they do not betray each other in this respect, even though Comrade Ossipon directed shamelessly inviting glances towards Winnie. Verloc provides Winnie with a home which is not less than she deserves. He provides for Stevie and Winnie's mother without a murmur of discontent. Indeed, his generosity seems virtually transcendental to Winnie's mother. She wishes to reduce his burden by entering an almshouse and thereby secure permanent provision for Stevie, though Verloc had not said or done anything to warrant her self-sacrifice and anxiety on account of her son. On the other hand, Winnie is a dutiful wife. She not only runs the household efficiently, lends a hand in the shop, but is solicitous for Verloc's welfare; here is the scene at night in the bedroom of the Verlocs after Verloc had been upset by his encounter with Mr. Vladimir at the Russian embassy:

> Mrs. Verloc expressed her surprise at seeing him up yet.
>
> "I don't feel very well", he muttered, passing his hands over his moist brow.
>
> "Giddiness ?"
>
> "Yes. Not at all well."
>
> Mrs. Verlac, with all the placidity of an experienced wife, expressed a confident opinion as to the cause, and suggested the usual remedies: but her husband, rooted in the middle of the room, shook his lowered head sadly.
>
> "You'll catch cold standing there," she abserved. (p 57)

Winnie's conscientiousness answers to Verloc's own conscientiousness and is less worthy his Hers derives partly from gratitude for Verloc's generosity in providing for Stevie and her mother, where as his is entirely on her own account.

The relationship of Verloc and Winnie is catapulted into a crisis when Stevie dies in the bomb blast. The manner in which this crisis is presented, illustrates Conrad's mastery of a modernist form for his novel. The pivot of the entire plot is only one incident, Verloc's attempt to blow up the Greenwich Observatory, and Conrad so uses it that it is perfectly adequate for such a complex and rich novel. As early as chapter four, during the conversation between Comrade Ossipon and the Professore, Conrad mentions the explosion at Greenwich Park and Verloc's association with it, but it is only towards the end of chapter nine that a clear picture of the incidents emerges. In-between Conrad employs cunning shifts of time and the climactic last scene between Verloc and Winnie gains maximum intensity and maximum ironic import.

It is true that Verloc had employed Stevie to carry the bomb with which he accidentally blew himself up, and Verloc had hidden from Stevie the real nature of his assignment. He had betrayed

Stevie's trust in him as the soul of wisdom and goodness and also Winnie's belief in him as a generous, selfless patron, she had even regarded him as Stevie's faster father. But Verloc remains, as Conrad himself states in the novel, "a human being—and not a monster as Mrs. Verloc believed him to be." (p. 257) It was impossible for Verloc to take Stevie into his confidence because the lad was a half-wit. Moreover, Verlac tells Winnie :

> "By heavens! You know that I hunted high and low. I ran the risk of giving myself away to find somebody for that accursed job. And I tell you again I couldn't find any one crazy enough or hungry enough. What do you take me for—a murderer, or what ? The boy is gone. Do you think I wanted him to blow himself up ? He's gone. His troubles are over. Ours are just going to begin, I tell you. But just try to understand that it was a pure accident, as much an accident as if he had been run over by a bus while crossing the street." (pp. 256-7)

Of course, Stevie's death is not quite "a pure accident, as much an accident as if he had been run over by a bus while crossing the street" and Verloc is responsible for employing Stevie on a dangerous and unlawful mission, absolutely outside the normal course of Stevie's life. But three is something to be said for the circumstances which Verloc mentions; these are extenuating. Whereas Verloc truthfully says "I didn't mean any harm to come to the boy" (p. 231), Winnie is incapable of judging him properly and proceeds to misjudge him.

> Mrs. Verloc's mental condition had the merit of simplicity, but it was not sound. It was governed to much by a fixed idea. Every nook and cranny of her brain was filled with the thought that this man, with whom she had lived without distaste for seven years, had taken the "poor boy" away from her in order to kill him—the man to whom she had grown accustomed in body and mind; the man whom she had trusted, took the boy away to kill him! (p. 249)

Verloc appears fully human in being driven to desperation by Mr. Vladimir's forcefully expressed threat to discontinue his service as a spy of the Russian embassy if he did not commit an outrage that would influence the British government to pass repressive legislation.

Verloc felt, quite rightly, that his whole livelihood was being menaced. He attempts to save himself *and* Winnie by trying to blow up the Greenwich Obsesvatory; his motive is understandably human and not wholly selfish. When he tells his wife, "Do be reasonable, Winnie. What would it have been if you lost me ?" (p. 234), he has grounds to feel aggrieved. He genuinely sympathises with Winnie in her bereavement and tries to console her :

> "You'll have to pull yourself together, my girl", he said, sympathetically, "What's done can't be undone."
>
> Mrs. Verloc gave a slight start, though not a muscle of her white face moved in the least. Mr. Verloc, who was not looking at her, continued ponderously:
>
> "You go to bed now. What you want is a good cry." (pp. 240-41)

During the crisis, Verloc's feelings and thoughts range from fatalism ("Nothing could be helped now" p. 231), to generous sympathy for Winnie, annoyance at her stupor and even to optimism. He looks forward to life after serving a term of imprisonment and, with characteristic generosity of spirit, he includes Winnie in his plans for the future. He is open about his secret life in a way he had never been. Yet none of Verloc's moods or words elicit a proper response from Winnie or alter her obsession that he had intentionally murdered Stevie. Her reactions to the crisis are independent of Verloc's and have a much narrower range, She moves from a nightmarish paralysis of rage and despair over Stevie's death to a murderous cunning and a macabre sense of irresponsibility and idleness. The vagueness and superficiality of the relationship of the Verlocs and the insu'ation between them, which were responsible for the success of their marriage, is also responsible for its failure. Understanding and communication are needed during the crisis if the marriage is to survive, and these are precluded by the very nature of their relationship. Verloc was incapable of understanding "either the nature or the whole extent of" Winnie's passion for Stevie (p. 233), while Winnie had been incapable of cnmmunicating this passion to Verlcc. She is incapable of understanding Verloc or joining him in a search for a solution to their difficult problem. The crisis jolts Verloc into making gestures of understanding and communication, but these are not reciprocated by Winnie. When her obsession compels her to plunge a carving-knife into Verloc, the reader does not feel that justice is being done. It seems to me that Winnie is more to blame than Verloc for the final collapse of their marriage and our sympathies, at this stage in the novel, are with Verloc rather than with Winnie. Still, Winnie never loses our sympathy. Verloc's case is complicated and it is difficult for her to judge him, especially in her emotional state. Indeed, it is difficult even for a person better endowed intellectually than Winnie and without her emotional involvement to judge Verloc's case. Our sympathies for her increase when she flees alter murdering Verloc. She entrusts herself and her money to Comrade Ossipon, only to be detrayed. She believes that Ossipon loves her for her own sake, ironically recalling to the reader Verloc's belief that Winnie loved him in his own right, whereas Ossipon is interested only in her money. He gets hold of her money and then deserts her. She commits suicide soon after. Yet Ossipon is not a monster. His increased disinclination to assist Winnie after he discovers the murder, is human and understandable. He feels guilty when he learns of Winnie's suicide and his own personality disintegrates. His plight adds to the pathos of the novel's conclusion.

The story, then, is as much Verloc's as Winnie's. If she is the "heroine," then she is not the single chief character. In this case, Verloc is the "hero" and an equally important character. Indeed, the terms "hero" and "heroine" are not quite appropriate when applied to Verloc and Winnie. Both are not heroic and do not win our wholehearted sympathy and approval. Rather, Verloc is an anti-hero and Winnie an anti-heroine. Our sympathies and approval for both are divided and well up in much the same degree, for both. If there is a difference of degree, it is in Verloc's favour. The value of their relationship is nil and it ends in disaster, in nothing. Winnie precariously holds on to a love of life after murdering Verloc, but this is soon crushed and is not established as a positive value. Conrad's outlook, then, in his presentation of the personal themes is completely sceptical.

In his valuable pages on *The Secret Agent in The Great Tradition*, F.R. Leavis is preoccupied with Conrad's moral interest in the novel. But it seems to me that Conrad has a distinctly social interest which Leavis neglects. There is a social theme about order and disorder which is important and bulks large in the novel. In fact, the personal and social themes are interrelated: Verloc's public role as a double agent is partly responsible for his personal isolation at home; the attempt to blow up the Greenwich Observatory represents an attempt made by Verloc to save both his public profession and private home and, ironically, the attempt results in the destruction of both. The social theme is presented with the same kind of art as the personal theme; see, for instance, the scene at the Russian embassy, early in the book:

> Mr. Vladimir bore the look of heavy inquiry with perfect serenity.
>
> "What we want is to administer a tonic to the Conference in Milan," he said, alrily. "Its deliberations upon international action for the suppression of political crime don't seem to get anywhere. England lags. This country is absurd with its sentimental regard for individual liberty. It's intolerable to think that all your friends have got only to come over to."
>
> "In that way I have them all under my eye," Mr. Verloc interrupted, huskily.
>
> "It would be much more to the point to have them all under lock and key. England must be brought into line. The imbecile bourgeoisie of this country make themselves the accomplices of the very people whose aim is to drive them out of their houses to starve in ditches. And they have the political power still, if they only had the sense to use it for their preservation. I suppose you agree that the middle classes are stupid ?"
>
> "Mr. Verloc hoarsely.
>
> "They are."
>
> "They have no imagination. They are blinded by an idiotic vanity. What they want just now is a jolly good scare. This is the psychological moment to set your friends to work. I have had you called here to develop to you my idea."

"A series of outrages," Mr. Vladimir continued calmly, "executed here in this country; not only *planned* here—that would not do—they would not mind. Your friends could set half the Continent on fire without influencing the public opinion here in favour of a universal repressive legislation. They will not look outside their backyard here."

Mr. Verloc cleared his throat, but his heart failed him, and he said nothing, (pp. 29-30).

Verloc is aware of the ironies of his position: he is conscious of the real difficulties of his job in a way Vladimir is not and does not care about Above both the characters operates the still wiser irony of Conrad. His irony shows up, by implication, the ineptness of Verloc, the unscrupulousness and brutal repression of autocracy represented by Vladimir, and the perverse destructiveness of anarchism. Conrad's irony also suggests that there is some truth in Vladimir's criticism of English insularity and middle-class denseness, but at the same time it suggests that the present state of order in England with its "individual liberty" is wrongfully menaced and is to be preferred to autocracy and anarchism. The irony thus works at several levels at the same time, and packs a wealth of social and political insight into the comic scene.

Conrad's sceptical insight is so penetrating that the social theme takes the reader to the very core of social and political realities of a capitalist state. These are thoughts evoked in Chief Inspector Heat when he runs into the Professor in a London street:

Chief Inspector Heat was, of course, not insensible to the gravity of moral differences. But neither were the thieves he had been looking after. They submitted to the severe sanctions of a morality familiar to Chief Inspector Heat with a certain resignation. They were his fellow-citizens gone wrong because of imperfect education, Chief Inspector Heat believed; but allowing for that difference, he could understand the mind of a burglar, because as a matter of fact, the mind and the instincts of a burglar are of the same kind as the mind and the instincts of a police officer. Both recognize the same conventions, and have a working knowledge of each other's methods and of the routine of their respective trades. They understand each other, which is advantageous to both, and establishes a short of amenity in their relations. Products of the same machine, one classed as useful and the other as noxious, they take the machine for granted in different ways, but with a seriousness essentially the same. The mind of Chief Inspector Heat was inaccessible to ideas of revolt. But his thieves were not rebels. His bodily vigour, his cool, inflexible manner, his courage, and his fairness, had secured for him much respect and some adulation in the sphere of his early successes. He had felt himself revered and admired. And Chief Inspector Heat, arrested within six paces of the anarchist nick-named the Professor, gave a thought of regret to the world of thieves—sane, without morbid ideals, working by routine, respectful of constituted authorities, free from all taint of hate and despair.

After paying the tribute to what is normal in the constitution of society (for the idea of thieving appeared to his instinct as normal as the idea of property), Chief Inspector Heat felt very angry with himself for having stopped, for having spoken, for having taken that way at all on the ground of it being a short cut from the station to the headquarters. (pp. 92-3)

Conrad suggests ironies at the centre of the situation. He sees law and crime, property and thieving, as two sides of the same coin and anarchism in this system as both peculiar and insanely destructive. Conrad is also indignant at Heat's calm acceptance of the given social state. Conrad's many-faceted irony plays on Heat as a representative of order, on ordinary society and on anarchism. More striking, artistically, is the scene when Winnie and Stevie converse after leaving behind the wretched cabman, the equally wretched horse and the cab in which Winnie's mother had been conveyed to the almshouse:

Hanging back suddenly, Stevie inflicted an arresting jerk upon his sister.

"Poor! Poor!" he ejaculated, appreciatively. "Cabman poor, too. He told me himself."

The contemplation of the infirm and lonely steed overcame him. Jostled, but obtinate, he would remain there, trying to express the view newly opened to his sympathies of the human and equine misery in close association. But it was very difficult. "Poor brute, poor people!" was all he could repeat. It did not seem forcible enough, and he came to a stop with an angry splutter: "Shame!" Stevie was no master of phrases, and perhaps for that very reason his thoughts lacked clearness and precision. But he felt with greater completeness and some-profundity. That little word contained all his sense of indignation and horror at one sort of wretchedness having to feed upon the anguish of the other—at the poor cabman beating the poor horse in the name, as it were, of his poor kids at home. And Stevie knew that it was to be beaten. He knew it from experience. It was a bad world. Bad! Bad!

Mrs. Verloc, his only sister, guardian, and protector, could not pretend to such depths of insight. Moreover, she had not experienced the magic of the cabman's eloquence. She was in the dark as to the inwardness of the word "Shame". And she said placidly:

"Come along, Stevie. You can't help that".

The docile Stevie went along; but now he went along without pride, shamblingly, and muttering half words, and even words that would have been whole if they had not been made up of halves that did not belong to each other. It was as though he had been trying to fit all the words he could remember to his sentiments in order to get some sort of corresponding idea. And, as a matter of fact, he got it at last. He hung back to utter it at once.

"Bad world for poor people".

"Don't you know what the police are for, Stevie? They are there so that them as have nothing shouldn't take anything away from them who have".

She avoided using the verb "to steal", because it always made her brother uncomfortable. For Stevie was delicately honest. Certain simple principles had been instilled into him so anxiously (on account of his "queerness") that the mere names of certain transgressions filled him with horror. He had been always easily impressed by speeches. He was impressed and startled now, and his intelligence was very alert.

"What ?" he asked at once, anxiously. "Not even if they were hungry ? Mustn't they ?"

The two had paused in their walk.

"Not if they were ever so," said Mrs. Verloc, with the equanimity of a person untroubled by the problem of the distribution of wealth, and exploring the perspective of the roadway for an omnibus of the right colour. "Certainly not. But what's the use of talking about all that ? You aren't ever hungry," (pp. 170-74)

The scene is fine ironic comedy. Conrad sees to it that the thoughts and speech of Stevie and Winnie are perfectly in character and at the same time suggests insights beyond their minds. Stevie's sympathy for the poor is, in the main, inarticulate and naively instinctive and Winnie's resignation to the existence of poverty is superficial, yet Conrad also suggests central problems of capitalist society, the inequality of classes and the distribution of wealth.

Irving Howe regards Conrad as a conservative,[9] but it seems to me that in *The Secret Agent*, Conrad is not a conservative but a "critical realist," to use a term from Soviet literary criticism. Arnold Kettle notes, "By *Critical Realism* I assume we mean literature written in the era of class society from a point of view which, while not fully socialist, is nevertheless sufficiently critical of class society to reveal important truths about that society and to contribute to the freeing of the human consciousness from the limitations which class society has imposed on it."[10] *The Secret Agent* was written in the era of class society. Conrad was not a socialist; we may recall that the socialist who enters *Nostromo* at the close of the novel is a gross caricature. Yet Conrad is sufficiently critical of class society to reveal important truths about that society, as regards both personal and social life, and by his unflinching exposure of these truths, he contributes to the freeing of human consciousness from the limitations which class society has imposed on it. While pointing to deficiencies and problems of capitalist society, Conrad at the same time suggests that it is greatly preferable to the autocracy of Czarist Russia and anarchism. And the preference is sound.

In England, anarchism was a movement of minor consequence. As George Woodcock notes,

> English anarchism has never been anything else than a chorus of voices crying in the wilderness, though some of the voices have been remarkable. At no time did the anarchists have even a remote chance of controlling the British labour movement. They have always been a small sect, hardly existent outside London and Glasgow, and in adapting themselves to their situation without admitting it, they have concentrated more than libertarians in many other countries on the graces of art and intellect.[11]

If Conrad was principally interested in English anarchism in its own right, a part of the subject of *The Secret Agent* would have been of minor significance. But fortunately Conrad is concerned with anarchism not so much as a movement in its own right, but as a form of social disorder. As such, he does not attempt to evaluate anarchism as a movement ; it is irrelevant to criticise Conrad for neglecting "the real and most impressive best" among the 19th century anarchists as Irving Howe does.[12] It is true that, as George Woodcock notes, "the modest record of the English movement shows an experimental spirit which has embraced every kind of anarchist thought and has produced every type of anarchist individual, with the sole exception of the practising terrorist."[13] But Conrad does not intend to present or suggest or do justice to the range of English anarchist thought or of English anarchist individuals. He has selected four types of anarchists—Karl Yundt, Comrade Ossipon, the Professor ond Michaelis—who, though not representing the best among the anarchists, still seem to me convincingly lifelike rank-and-file social rebels. They are presented as bold caricatures and their repelling physical attributes reflect Conard's moral disapproval.

Karl Yundt is a preacher of terrorism and his distinguishing feature in this respect was that "he took the part of an insolent and venomous evoker of sinister impulses which lurk in the blind envy and exasperated vanity of ignorance, in the suffering and misery of poverty, in all the hopeful and noble illusions of righteous anger pity, and revolt." (p. 48) He is disgustingly decrepit. He was "old and bald, with a narrow, snow white wisp of a goatee hanging limply from his chin ;" his mouth was "toothless," his eyes were "extinguished," his "skinny groping hand deformed by gouty swellings." (p. 42) Comrade Ossipon is a pamphleteer and he thinks : "the only thing that matters to us is the emotional state of the masses. Without emotion there is no action." (p. 50) Though he lives off the women he seduces, he is curiously wanting in attractions : "a bush of crinkly yellow hair topped his red, freckled face, with a flattened nose and prominent mouth cast in the rough mould of the negro type." (p. 44) "The negro types" of Ossipon's features is meant by Conrad to denote ugliness. The Professor feels superior to the other revolutionists because he is more dangerous : he dabbles in explosives and carries with him a bomb that could wipe out every creature in his vicinity. His ideas are more deadly then those of the others :

> "To break up the superstition and worship of legality should be our aim. Nothing would please me more than to see Inspector Heat and his likes take to shooting us down in broad daylight with the approval of the public. Half our battle would be won then ; the disintegration of the old morality would have set in its very temple. That is what you ought to aim at. But you revolutionists will never understand that. You plan the future, you lose yourselves in reveries of economical systems derived from what is ; whereas what's wanted is a clean sweep and a clear start for a new conception of life. That short of future will take care of itself if you will only make room for it. Therefore I would shovel my stuff in heaps at the corners of the streets if I had enough for that;

and as I haven't, I do my best by perfecting a really dependable detonator." (p. 73).

The Professor's appearance is unprepossessing. He is puny, frail and shabby ; "his flat large ears departed widely from the sides of his skull......the flat cheeks, of a greasy, unhealthy complexion, were merely smudged by the miserable poverty of a thin dark whisker." (p. 62) Michaelis is presented as the least objectionable of the anarchists. Conrad is capable of seeing to it that Michaeilis lucidly, accurately and consistently expresses Marxism :

> "......All idealization makes life poorer. To beautify it is to take away its character of complexity—it is to destroy it. Leave that to the moralists, my boy. History is made by men, but they do not make it in their heads. The ideas that are born in their consciousness play an insignificant part in the march of events. History is dominated and determined by the tool and the production—by the force of economic conditions. Capitalism has made socialism, and the laws made by the capitalism for the protection of property are responsible for anarchism. No one can tell what form the social organization may take in the future. Then why indulge in prophetic phantasies ? At best they can only interpret the mind of the prophet, and can have no objective value. Leave that pastime to the moralists, my boy." (p. 41).

Conrad's condemnation of Michaelis too is clearly implied in the physical attributes which he gives the ticket-of leave apostle :

> He had come out of a highly hygienic prison round like a tub, with an enormous stomach and distended cheeks of a pale, semitransparent complexion, as though for fifteen years the servants of an outraged society had made a point of stuffing him with fattening foods in a damp and lightless cellar (p. 41).

The anarchists are not, however, totally revolting. It is customary for critics to overlook the sympathy which Conrad elicits for the anarchists by sketching their past to explain their present state and by other suggestions. The Professor is, as Conrad indicates in a letter, "a megalomaniac of an extreme type,"[14] but even from him I do not wholly recoil. Conrad makes us understand how the frustration of the Professor's ambition and vanity influences him to formulate destruction as his creed ;[15] we respect his peculiar integrity ; we feel sorry for the way he is lost in crowds and is undersized, miserable and lonely. Our sympathies go out to Michaelis when we learn that his term of imprisonment is not justified, that it has made him obese and, much worse, damaged his mind. Yet far more important than Conrad's sympathy for the anarchists is his criticism. All of them serve to bring out, in common, "the criminal futility of the whole thing, doctrine, action, mentality" and "the contemptible aspect of the half-crazy pose as of a brazen cheat exploiting the poignant miseries and passionate credulities of a mankind always so tragically eager for self-destruction."[16]

In *The Secret Agent*, the forces of disorder are opposed by forces of order. Conrad sees ironies in the forces of order too. "Chief Inspector Heat was a kind man, an excellent husband, a devoted father ;" he enjoyed "public and departmental confidence." (p. 119) But he could be shockingly dishonest and unjust : he wanted to frame Michaelis for the explosion at Greenwich Park. He uses Verloc as an informer unknown to anyone else in his department and he wanted to hide this fact even when it interferes with the true investigation of the explosion. He conceals the address tab he found under the lapel of dead Stevie's coat until the Assistant Commissioner forces out the information. There seems to be some truth in the Assistant Commissioner's fleeting thought that the reputation of Chief Inspector Heat might possibly have been made in a great part by the Secret Agent Verloc." (p. 131) Thus, Conrad suggests the existence of dubious methods and incongruities behind the smooth public front of Justice. His moral disapproval of Heat is implicit in his description of Heat's physiognomy as having "too much flesh." (p. 116) When we discuss the Assistant Commissioner, we remember A.J. Guerard's true contention that "such slight author-identification as exists in *The Secret Agent* is clearly with Assistant Commissioner."[17] Yet the more important thing is that Conrad is able to portray him with sufficient objectivity so as to place him. He had "considerable gifts for detection" (p. 117) and he is more than a match for Heat. He, not Heat, finds out from Verloc that Vladimir had instigated the bomb outrage. Yet he feels uncomfortable in his present job ; he dislikes being "chained to a desk in the thick of four millions of men" (p. 113) whereas, in contrast, "the police-work he had been engaged on in a distant part of the globe had the saving character of an irregular sort of warfare or at least the risk and excitement of open-air sport." (pp. 112-13) He is impelled, in the first place, to save Michaelis from Heat's inclination to frame him, not from a sense of justice, but from self-interest ; he does not wish to offend Michaelis' aristocratic patroness because she was a "good friend" of his wife and himself (p. 112) and had an "excellent influence" upon his wife. (pp. 111-12) Still, he is the least objectionable among the representatives of order ; naturally, he is lean and his appearance is unoffending. The elder statesman's appearance implies the Conrad disapproves of him more strongly :

> Vast in bulk and stature, with a long white face, which, broadened at the base by a big bouble chin, appeared egg-shaped in the fringe of thin greyish whisker, the great personage seemed an expanding man. Unfortunate from a tailoring point of view, the cross-folds in the middle of a buttoned black coat added to the impression, as if he fastenings of the garment were tried to the utmost. From the head, set upward on a thick neck, the eyes, with puffy lower lids, stared with a haughty droop on each side of a hooked, aggressive nose, nobly salient in the vast pale circumference of the face. (p. 136)

He is self-centred and conducts himself with a sense of self-importance, yet he is not corrupt. His private secretary is silly, bumptious, and has been appointed purely because of his social status, regardless of merit. In sum, the representative of order in *The Secret Agent* are not as reprehensible as the representatives of disorder, but they are tainted.

One critical issue remains : the question of setting. London is presented with a Dickensian vividnes and vitality, also with less caricature and more realism than in Dickens. Probably, it is the effectiveness of Conrad's portrayal of London that prompted Leo Gurko to elaborate an eccentric thesis that "the heart of the book, the dominant idea that determines its movement, is London."[18] Numerous touches—for instance, Conrad writes: "on the pavement of the squalid and wide throughfare, whose poverty in all the amenities of life stood foolishly exposed by a mad profusion of gas-lights, . . ." (p. 170)—build up a total composite impression of London as a sprawling murky sordid metropolis. Not only the personal theme and the social theme, Conrad's presentation of the setting too is disillusioned. His disillusion is unflinching and total. His vision in *The Secret Agent* is fully modernistic.

NOTES

1. Joseph Conrad, 'Author's Note' (1917): *Nostromo,* London: Penguin, 1963 ed., p. 12.
2. C.T. Watts (ed.), *Joseph Conrad's Letters to R.B. Cunninghame Graham*, Cambridge: The University Press, 1969, p. 169.
3. See D.C.R.A. Goonetilleke, *Developing Countries in British Fiction*, London, Macmillan, 1977, p. 110.
4. F.R. Leavis, *The Great Tradition,* London: Penguin, 1962 ed., p. 231.
5. Joseph Conard, *The Secret Agent,* London: Dent, 1961 ed., p. 4; all later quotations from the novel are from this edition and their page numbers are noted in my text.
6. Conrad, 'Author's Preface' (1920): *The Secret Agent*, p. xii.
7. Christopher Cooper, *Conrad and the Human Dilemma*, London: Chatto & Windus, 1970, p. 19.
8. Christopher Cooper, op. cit., p. 19.
9. Irving Nowe, *Politics and the Novel*, Cleveland & N.Y.: World Publishing Company, 1962 ed., p. 79.
10. Arnold Kettle, "Dickens and the Popular Tradition," David Craig (ed.), *Marxists on Literature*, London: Penguin, 1975, p. 214.
11. George Woodcock, *Anarchism*, London : Penguin, 1972 ed , p. 414.

12. Irving Nowe, *op. cit*, pp. 97-8.
13. George Woodcock, *op. cit*, p 415.
14. Joseph Conrad, letter to R.B. Cunninghame Graham, 7 October 1907 : C.T. Watts (ed.), *Letters to Cunninghame Graham*, p. 170.
15. See especially *The Secret Agent*, pp. 80-1.
16. Conrad, 'Author's Preface' : *The Secret Agent*, p. ix.
17. A J Guerard, *Conrad the Novelist*, Cambridge, Massachusetts : Harvard University Press, 1962, p. 223.
18. Lee Gurko, *Joseph Conrad : Giant in Exile*, N.Y. Macmillan, 1962, p. 169.

CHAPTER 13

Conrad's Victory Reconsidered

Greater Britain furnishes a convenient limbo for damaged characters and careers.

—J.A. Hobson, *Imperialism : A Study*

Conrad was not very well understood in his time, and it is a mordant comment on the quality of the reading public that one of the great writers of the world found it extremely difficult to live by his pen during his prime (from 1901 to 1911). Even Virginia Woolf, in her obituary essay (1924), said :

> Therefore, though we shall make expeditions into the later books and bring back wonderful trophies, large tracts of them will remain by most of us untrodden It is the earlier books—*Youth, Lord Jim, Typhoon, The Nigger of the 'Narcissus'*—that we shall read in their entirety. For when the question is asked, what of Conrad will survive and where in the ranks of novelists we are to place him, these books, with their air of telling us something very old and perfectly true, which had lain hidden but is now revealed, will come to mind and make such questions and comparisons seem a little futile. Complete and still, very chaste and very beautiful, they rise in the memory as, on these hot summer nights, in their slow and stately way first one star comes out and them another.[1]

It was F.R. Leavis, in his articles in *Scrutiny* (1941), who pioneered acutely discriminating criticism of Conrad's fiction. He argued that Conrad had written valuable tales with sea settings and that his greatness rested mainly on his later novels, *Nostromo, The Secret Agent, Under Western Eyes, Chance* and *Victory.*[2] Although I do not wholly endorse Leavis's analysis or regard it is complete in essentials, I am very much in agreement with his basic judgement of *Nostromo, The Secret Agent* and *Under Western Eyes.* But is *Victory*, as Leavis says, "among those of Conrad's works which deserve to be current as representing his claim to classical standing" ?[3] Or, is a more recent minority view (held by critics like Albert J. Guerard and Douglas Hewitt) correct, is the novel "very badly written and very roughly imagined" ?[4]

The "undeveloped" world of *Victory* is the same as that of *Almayer's Folly*, *An Outcast of the Islands*, *Lord Jim* and *The Rescue* ; it is like that of *Nostromo*. Axel Heyst, like Willems and Lord Jim, is virtually a protagonist. But unlike in the case of Willems and Lord Jim, all those who play a decisive role in his drama are Europeans—his father, Morrison, Lena and the desperadoes. The Malayans are referred to as part of the background, but they never come on stage. Indeed, *Victory* is unique among the Malayan novels in this respect. The only "coloured" characters who appear as *dramatis personae* are the three Chinese immigrants.

Heyst's character is strikingly dissimilar to all Canrad's earlier Europeans in the Malay Archipelago. He scorns mankind.

> Heyst was not conscious of either friends or of enemies. It was the very essence of his life to be a solitary achievement, accomplished not by hermit-like withdrawal with its silence and immobility, but by a system of restless wandering, by the detachment of an impermanent dweller amongst changing scenes. In this scheme he had perceived the means of passing through life without suffering and almost without a single care in the world—invulnerable because elusive.[5]

Thus when he goes to Samburan, he is not running away from life but coping with it in a peculiar way. His extreme scepticism, like that of Decoud in *Nostromo*, goes with rootlessness ; and in this way, both of them bear affinities to Conrad's own sensibility. Moreover, in the case of Heyst, to these is added isolation, another condition familiar to Conrad. Thus, he is particularly close to the author. True insight makes Conrad place Heyst in an "undeveloped" region ; as J.A. Hobson puts it, "Greater Britain furnished a convenient limbo for damaged characters "[6] Heyst does not recover from the damage caused to his mind when young by the influence of his deeply unhappy, cynical father, and he comes to the East with his damaged mind.

A convincing impression of "white" colonial society in the tropics is created by the accumulation of a wealth of authentic features ; there are the white suits, cork helmets and pipe-clayed white shoes of the Europeans ; there is the apartheid in Schomberg's hotel. But Heyst lives, not in this exclusive society of Sourabaya, but on a distant island without any company until he takes Lena there A part of his drama takes place in Sourabaya, but most of it in Samburan. Conrad's central concern in *Victory* is with Heyst's affairs. Thus the success of the novel depends on his presentation of Heyst's drama, not on his evocation of European society in Sourabaya.

The key to Heyst's plight lies in these words of the anonymous narrator of the early phases of *Victory*.

> . . . his detachment from the world was not complete. And incompleteness of any sort leads to trouble. (p. 23)

What essentially makes Heyst vulnerable is an humanity which has not been killed by his scepticism. This goes out to decent people in distress and makes him appreciate worthiness : it leads to ties with certain people. His first relationship is with Morrison. He pities the unbusinesslike trader and helps him financially. He is unable to resist participation in Morrison's activities and even becomes "the manager on the spot of the Tropical Belt Coall Company, with offices in London and Amsterdam" (p. 13) His humanity extends to "undeveloped" countries :

> We doubted whether he had any visions of wealth — for himself, at any rate. What he seemed mostly concerned for was the "stride forward," as he expressed it, in the general organisation of the universe, apparently. He was heard by more than a hundred persons in the islands talking of a "great stride forward for these regions." (p. 3)

He is idealistic in a conventionally Victorian optimistic way, but his motives win our respect ; they are the reverse of Almayer's and Willems's greed. His involvements meet with disaster : Morrison dies before long on a visit to England and the Tropical Belt Coal Company goes into liquidation soon. Heyst detaches himself from "facts" again, but these setbacks leave their mark : he feels "a sort of shame before his own betrayed nature" ; he suffers absurdly from "remorse" over Morrison's death and from a new "sense of loneliness" (pp. 51, 52). His appreciative kindness remains : he confesses to Davidson, "I am touched by your humanity", because he "understood in a proper sense the little *Sissie's* periodical appearance in sight of his hermitage" after his reversals (p. 25).

These episodes, indeed all episodes of the first part of the novel, are rendered efficiently. Heyst comes alive dramatically as a complex and developing character. But our interest flickers when his relationship with Lena occupies the centre of the stage. This is the first time that Conrad is presenting a relationship between a "white" man and a "white" woman in an "undeveloped" country. It brings about the more important developments in Heyst and, indeed, forms the body of the drama. His humanity makes him pity Lena, and she is glad to be rescued from Zangiacomo's orchestra. Their feelings for each other at the beginning are very romantic and this is plausible given their respective circumstances : though thirty-five years old, Heyst has not as yet become friendly with any woman and Lena appeals to him ; Lena has suffered from miseries since childhood ; Heyst is her rescuer and he is a distinguished person. Consider one of the interesting scenes, the scene in Heyst's house in Samburan just before Wang announces the arrival of the desperadoes :

> "Tired, are you ! It's my fault, taking you up so high and keeping you out so long. Such a windless day, too!"
>
> She watched his concern, her pose languid, her eyes raised to him, but as unreasonable as ever. He avoided looking into them for that very reason. He forgot himself in the contemplation of those passive arms, of these defenceless lips, and—yes one had to go back to them—of these wide open eyes. Something wild in their grey stare made him think of seabirds in the cold murkiness of high latitudes. He started when she spoke, all the charm of physical intimacy revealed suddenly in that voice.
>
> "You should try to love me !" she said.
>
> He had a movement of astonishment.

"Try !" he muttered. "But it seems to me—" He broke off, saying to himself that if he loved her, he had never told her so in so many words. Simple words ! They died on his lips. "What makes you say that ?" he asked.

She lowered her eyelids and turned her head a little.

"I have done nothing," she said in a low voice. "It's you who have been good, helpful, and tender to me. Perhaps you love me for that—just for that ; or perhaps you love me for company, and because—well ! But sometimes it seems to me that you can never love me for myself, only for myself, as people do love each other when it is to be for ever." Her head drooped. "For ever," she breathed out again ; then, still more faintly, she added an entreating : "Do try !"

These last words went straight to his heart—the sound of them more than the sense. He did not know what to say, either from want of practice in dealing with women, or simply from his innate honesty of thought. All his defences were broken now. Life had him fairly by the throat. But he managed a smile, though she was not looking at him ; yes, he did manage it—the well-known Heyst smile of playful courtesy, so familiar to all sorts and conditions of men in the islands.

"My dear Lena," he said, "it looks as if you were trying to pick a very unnecessary quarrel with me—of all people !"

She made no movement. With his elbows spread out, he was twisting the ends of his long moustaches, very masculine and perplexed, enveloped in the atmosphere of femininity as in a cloud, suspecting pitfalls, and as if afraid to move.

"I must admit though," he added, "that there is no one else ; and I suppose a certain amount of quarrelling is necessary for existence in this world."

That girl, seated in her chair in graceful quietude was to him like a script in an unknown language, or even more simply mysterious : like any writing to the illiterate. (pp. 176-7)

The attachment of Heyst and Lena as well as their want of complete fulfilment are conveyed with dramatic and descriptive power. Heyst's kind of embarrassment, introversion and impercipience are indicated by his movements such as "twisting the ends of his long moustaches", his "smile of playful courtesy", his urbane remonstrance and the final rather platitudinous rationalization which is self-consoling, peace-making and also evades the real problem. The sophistication of his speech fits the educated aristocrat. Now turn to Lena. Douglas Hewitt argues that her speech is "literary" that Conrad "can never catch the note of the uneducated" and that this is a major flaw in *Victory* because "it is essential for the effect of the book that we should see Lena as coming from a background of lodgings off the Kingsland Road, as having the naiveté of the uneducated waif, and yet as bringing love and faith to the intellectual and highly educated Heyst."[7] Of course, her way of speaking never resembles that of characters like Eliza Doolittle before her training under Professor Higgins, but it seems to me that Conrad usually gives her a simple living idiom which suits her and "the effect of the book". She is an uneducated working-class girl, but she has experience in higher social strata. Moreover, this does not serve to introduce her into Heyst's world, though they are not as extremely different as they would have been if she had remained stuck to her origins. The image of the "sea-birds" illuminates her present state and is in keeping with her hard life as a wanderer.

Still, Conrad's presentation of the Heyst-Lena relationship as it develops is vitiated by a conventional romanticism. The little use to which Conrad puts Lena's 'background' is usually in this vein : her miseries are brought in to add sentimentality ; her "purity" is incredible. One can scarcely believe that a girl such as Lena has had no sexual experience : she is a poor employee of cheap musical entertainments ; by her own admission, she is "not the sort that men turn their backs on" and "it isn't easy to stand up for yourself when you feel there's nothing and nobody at your back" (p. 68).

The final developments in their relationship and in Conrad's themes take place when the three desperadoes enter the drama. Jones bears a certain similarity to Gentleman Brown in *Lord Jim* who "was supposed to be the son of a baronet" ;[8] he claims to be a "gentleman". Both carry over into the criminal world something of the airs of their former "social sphere" (p. 301). But Jones is not violent as Brown is and, when violence is necessary, he directs his men to use it. The essential differences between Jones, Ricardo and Pedro are suggested by Heyst's description to Lena when she sees them for the first time from her bungalow :

> " . . . Here they are before you—evil intelligence, instinctive savagery, arm in arm. The brute force is at the back . . . " (p. 262).

But the desperadoes do not become symbols of these qualities. There are other similarly explicit attempts to endow them with a symbolic importance : Lena sees Ricardo as "the embodied evil of the world" (p. 237) ; Jones regards himself as "a sort of fate" (p. 301). An acceptable symbolic extension of meaning is almost impossible in their presentation because, in the first place, they do not come alive sufficiently as real human beings. Leavis thinks that they are "a kind of Morality representation, embodiments of counter-potentialities",[9] but it seems to me that Conrad does not follow allegorical modes as Leavis suggests. When Shakespeare depicts the witches in *Macbeth* he starts from contemporary popular belief and life, and presents them as embodiments of evil ; he does not attempt to make the witches human and they remain moral forces throughout the play. Conrad's villains, however, are not allegorical figures of this type. Nor do they resemble figures from a Morality play like *Everyman* : the writer of such a play commences with moral concepts and, then, tries to lend them human interest. Conrad's method of portraying the desperadoes is not allegorical but symbolic. He begins with human beings[10] and, then, tries to invest them with a symbolic moral significance. But his effort in this direction is a failure, as indicated above. M.C. Bradbrook is wrong to consider Jones "the Living Skeleton, the Heart of Darkness" ;[11] none of the criminals gains a serious symbolic significance. Still, because they are not exactly like the villains of popular melodramatic fiction, say, of Peter Cheynecy, Leslie Charteris of "Sapper", who begin from nothing but melodramatic convention and remain within this convention, they offer an human interest. It is marked in their early appearances in Schomberg's hotel :

> Schomberg tried to face the situation bravely, but that steady, black stare affected him. And when he glanced aside uncomfortably, he met Ricardo's grin uncovering a lot of teeth, though the man seemed absorbed in his thoughts all the time.
>
> "And, moreover," went on Mr. Jones in that distant tone of his, "you can't help yourself. Here we are and here we stay. Would you try to put us out ? I dare say you could do it ; but you couldn't do it without getting badly hurt – very badly hurt. We can promise him that, can't we, Martin ?"
>
> The Secretary retracted his lips and looked up sharply at Schomberg, as if only too anxious to leap upon him with teeth and claws.
>
> Schomberg managed to produce a deep laugh.
>
> "Ha ! Ha ! Ha !"
>
> Mr. Jones closed his eyes wearily, as if the light hurt them, and looked remarkably like a corpse for a moment. This was bad enough ; but when he opened them again, it was almost a worse trial for Schomberg's nerves. The spectral intensity of that glance, fixed on the hotel-keeper (and this was most frightful), without any definite expression, seemed to dissolve the last grain of resolution in his character.
>
> "You don't think, by any chance, that you have to do with ordinary people, do you ?" inquired Mr. Jones, in his lifeless manner, which seemed to imply some sort of menace from beyond the grave.
>
> "He's a gentleman" testified Martin Ricardo with a sudden snap of the lips, after which his moustaches stirred by themselves in an odd, feline manner. (pp. 88-9)

The "discomfiture" of the pusillanimous Schomberg and the breakdown of his "resolution" appear completely human. Jones's quietly menacing speech and demeanour and Ricardo's crude actions and sense of social inferiority are realized as fully as if they were part of any domestic scene, lurid though they could easily have become. Yet, generally speaking, Conrad's presentation of the desperadoes

does not come off. The key to Conrad's descriptions of all three desperadoes is found in Schomberg's reaction to them as "a spectre, a cat, an ape" (p. 118), and their actions are too often conceived within the framework of these three exaggerated analogies. This is partly why they soon begin to appear cardboard melodramatic caricatures rather than human criminals. Moreover as they play a larger role in *Victory* than all the other characters and as they play an important role in the denouement, the weakness in their presentation mars the novel more than any other.

When they reach Samburan, Heyst's character changes radically in response to demands unfamiliar to him. His attitude of scornful detachment falls off. He feels responsible for Lena and their relationship. He even cares for "what the world would say". He cannot put into action wily and brutal methods of defence, but he thinks of them after Wang stole his revolver.[12] Lena comes to feel that their only hope of safety lies in getting hold of Ricardo's knife. She tries to do this to prove her feelings for Heyst and to break through the "sense of incompleteness" in their love. She dies in the attempt, and her death scenes form the climax of the novel. Her death brings out ironically the novel's positive significance. It is useless as far as her relationship with Heyst or their lives as individuals are concerned (Heyst commits suicide soon after). At the same time, on her side, it is a victorious assertion of love—victorious because Heyst finally recognizes the full value of her love for him and of love as a valuable human quality in a general sense. On his side, it leads to this recognition of love and complementary qualities, to a final triumph over lifelong deep scepticism : these are "practically the last words he said to" Davidson.

> "Ah, Davidson, woe to the man whose heart has not learned while young to hope, to love,—and put its trust in life !" (p. 326)

Here Conrad, however, is putting the novel's positiveness in terms which are explicit, sentimental and unnecessary. The prominence of sentimentality and melodrama in the presentation of Heyst and Lena and their affairs reduce their lifelikeness and make especially

Lena a simplified character. The positive values are unexceptionably humane ; but these artistic weaknesses and the moral tag enfeeble their affirmation. In fact, Conrad's method of affirmation suggests that he is seeking ethical consolation rather than facing life whole and steadily ; this tendency forms a marked contrast to, say, the naked and unflinching disillusion of *The Secret Agent*.

Victory is a flawed but notable work. It is not a "classic", but nor can it be dismissed as "very badly written and very roughly imagined". It has a mixed value like that of E.M. Forster's pre-War novels.

NOTES

1. Virginia Woolf, "Joseph Conrad" (August 1924) : Leonard Woolf (ed.), *Collected Essays, Virginia Woolf*, London, 1966 ed., Vol. 1. pp. 307-8.

2. F.R. Leavis, *The Great Tradition*, London, 1962 ed., p. 247.

3. *Ibid.*, p. 230. Leavis' high opinion of *Victory* has not changed – Leavis, *Anna Karenina and other Essays*, London, 1967 ed., p. 95.

4. Albert J. Guerard, *Conrad the Novelist*, Massachusetts, 1962, p. 255 ; Douglas Hewitt, *Conrad : A Reassessment*, Cambridge, 1952, pp. 110-1. To G.S. Fraser, *Victory* seems "not much more than a first-rate melodrama" – Fraser, *The Modern Writer and his World*, London, 1964 ed., p. 88.

5. Conrad, *Victory*, London, 1954 ed., p. 72 ; all later quotations from the novel are from this edition and their page-numbers are noted in my test.

6. J.A. Hobson, *Imperialism : A Study*, London, 1938 ed., p. 51.

7. Douglas Hewitt, op. cit., pp. 109-10.

8. Conrad, *Lord Jim*, London, 1953 ed., p. 259.

9. Leavis, *The Great Tradition*, p. 229.

10. Conrad speaks of originals in life for his desperadoes in his "Author's Note" (1920) : *Victory*, London, 1960 ed pp xi-xv.

11. M.C. Bradbrook, *Joseph Conrad : Poland's English Genius*, New York, 1965 ed., p. 65.

12. See *Victory*, pp. 287-8.

CHAPTER 14

George Orwell's Burmese Days: the novelist as reformer

The truth is that no modern man, in his heart of hearts, believes that it is right to invade a foreign country and hold the population down by force.

—George Orwell, *The Road to Wigan Pier*

George Orwell has earned increasing respect as a thinker, essayist and moralist but, as a novelist, he continues to be undervalued. In 1940, Q.D. Leavis wrote :

Mr. Orwell must have wasted a lot of energy trying to be a novelist.

I think I must have read three or four novels by him, and the only impression these dreary books left on me is that nature didn't intend him to be a novelist.[1]

In 1976, Ian Hamilton says "Queenie was dead right"[2]. *Animal Farm* (1945) and *1984* (1949) have won some acclaim but Orwell's early fiction is at best viewed with affectionate tolerance. *Burmese Days* (1934) is his first novel and it has enjoyed a measure of popular readership.[3] Yet the critics generally underrate it[4] as Orwell himself did,[5] and they neglect it. Now our expectations of Orwell's early writing ought to be higher: his early pieces 'A Hanging' (1931) and 'Shooting an Elephant' (1936) are universally lauded as autobiographical essays but Bernard Crick recently suggested that Orwell may never have witnessed a hanging or shot an elephant[6]. It is doubtful whether these pieces are fact or fiction, yet their imaginative truth is undeniable and this suggests that Orwell was a better creative writer at an earlier stage than critics have generally conceded.

Burmese Days, then, is likely to be rewarding reading, and so it is. In his essay 'Why I Write' (1947), Orwell said: "What I have most wanted to do throughout the past ten years is to make political writing into an art. My starting-point is always a feeling of partisanship, a sense of injustice."[7] These are the impulses from which *Burmese Days* stems, though it was written earlier. It is clearly a political novel and begins from his sympathy for the Burmese. Orwell had spent five years (1922-7) in Burma as a member of the Indian Police (at that time, Burma was a part of the Raj) and had seen "the dirty work of Empire at close quarters."[8] Moreover, he tells F. Tennyson Jesse "Apart from my own time there I have family connexions with the country over three generations."[9] He himself had been born at Motihari, Bengal, in 1903 where his father was employed in the Opium Department of the Indian Civil Service. His paternal grandfather had served in the Indian army while his maternal grandfather had worked as a teak merchant in Burma. His personal connections with, and first-hand experience of the Raj lead him to an acute awareness that imperialism is "tyranny and exploitation,"[10] and in the novel he tries to show that "imperialism was a evil thing."[11] His intention is didactic; he is a reformer.

The whole novel is set in Burma during the days of the British Empire. The European characters in it are more important than the indigenous characters. In an imperial situation the importance of the 'ruling race' greatly exceeds their number and Orwell is right to present it as such. Let us consider a scene typical of this side of the novel—the discussion at the Club whether a native member should be elected :

> 'Is it quite playing the game,' he said stiffly, 'to call these people niggers—a term they very naturally resent—when they are obviously nothing of the kind ? The Burmese are Mongolians, the Indians are Aryans or Dravidians, and all of them are quite distinct . . .'
>
> 'Oh, rot that!' said Ellis, who was not at all awed by Mr. Macgregor's official status. 'Call them niggers or Aryans or what you like, what I'm saying is that we don't want to see

any black hides in this Club. If you put it to the vote you'll find we're against it to a man—unless Flory wants his *dear* pal Veraswami,' he added.

'Hear, hear!' repeated Mr. Lackersteen. 'Count on me to blackball the lot of 'em'.

....

'Our burra sahib at Mandalay always said,' put in Mrs. Lackersteen, 'that in the end we shall simply *leave* India. Young men will not come out here any longer to work all their lives for insults and ingratitude. We shall just *go*. When the natives come to us begging us to stay, we shall say, "No, you have had your chance, you wouldn't take it. Very well, we shall leave you to govern yourselves." And then, what a lesson that will teach them!'

'It's all this law and order that's done for us,' said Westfield gloomily. The ruin of the Indian Empire through too much legality was a recurrent theme with Westfield. According to him, nothing save a full-sized rebellion, and the consequent reign of martial law, could save the Empire from decay. 'All this paper-chewing and chit-passing'. Office babus are the real rulers of this country now. Our number's up. Best thing we can do is to shut up shop and let 'em stew in their own juice.'[12]

There can be no club in outposts like Conrad's Sambir and Patusan, but it was (to use Leonard Woolf's words) "a symbol and centre of British imperialism"[13] in places like Orwell's Kyauktada or E.M. Forster's Chandrapore. Orwell rightly presents it as such and focuses on it often in his presentation of the Europeans. The success of his drama derives from the firmness with which he holds his own humane values and from the accuracy, the sensitiveness with which he records their violation. The Anglo-Indians are shown as holding certain attitudes in common and, at the same time, they are carefully differentiated; each one has his or her distinctive voice. All are racialist but Mr. Macgregor is not virulent; he is condescending and tolerant. Ellis is belligerent, fanatical and malicious. Westfield is bloodthirsty and resigned. Both Mr. and Mrs. Lackersteen are stupid and superior but Mr. Lackersteen, unlike his wife, is without a back-bone, a hopeless drunkard and, we later find out, shamelessly lustful. The signs of the end of the Empire seem to lend their attitudes an edge absent in the Anglo-Indian characters in Kipling or Forster when the Empire was thriving. They conceal their self-interest behind a mask of altruism as Anglo-Indians did during the heyday of Empire, and, in addition, prepare for the final retreat with the same heartlessness with which they clung to power. In *A Passage to India,* Aziz tells Mrs. Moore at the end of their first encounter, 'Indians are not allowed into the Chandrapore Club even *as guests,*'[14] but in *Burmese Days* the pivot of the action is the question of the admission of a 'native' into the European club *as a member.* On the other hand, Burmese nationalism was not yet in full tide. The most important, highly placed and educated "native" characters in the novel are U Po Kyin and Dr. Varaswami. U Po Kyin is the Sub-divisional magistrate of Kyauktada. He holds the Europeans in much less awe than they were generally held during the heyday of Empire and he is not averse to making use of them to further himself. But he aspires to be a member of the European Club because membership carries prestige in his eyes and in the eyes of his society, not because he wants to make a dent in the armour of the British. He is not nationalistically inclined. Veraswami is an Indian doctor and he fanatically supports the British. He seeks admission to the Club because it carries prestige in his eyes and because it would make him less vulnerable to his enemy, U Po Kyin. Thus, the novel seems to be an authentic impression of a specific period of Burmese history, the 1920's. This particular period is suggested and the authenticity confirmed if we check the novel more closely against actual history. Burma was excluded from the Government of India Act of 1919 which introduced dyarchy and other reforms to India. The Burmese retaliated with mass agitation lead by monks and students. Dyarchy reforms, which included desegregation of European Clubs and recruitment of "natives" into senior positions, were extended to Burma in 1923. The British regarded these as substantial concessions, but they did not satisfy the Burmese who struggled until they achieved independence in 1948.

All the Anglo-Indians in *Burmese Days*—with the exception of Flory—are rather simple characters and they come alive. Indeed, their characterisation borders on caricature yet is nevertheless fully realistic. Orwell suggests that the Europeans in the colonies are, in fact, caricatures of human beings rather than normal people. Their characters are moulded by the code of the pukka sahibs; its "five chief beatitudes" are :

> Keeping up our prestige,
> The firm hand (without the velvet glove),
> We white men must hang together,
> Give them an inch and they'll take an ell, and
> Esprit de Corps.
>
> (p. 181)

The Anglo-Indians lack the personal freedom to be anything but sahibs. As a part of his authorial commentary, Orwell wrote :

> It is a stifling, stultifying world in which to live. It is a world in which every word and every thought is censored. In England it is hard even to imagine such an atmosphere. Everyone is free in England; we sell our souls in public and buy them back in private, among our friends. But even friendship can hardly exist when every white man is a cog in the wheels of despotism. Free speech is unthinkable. All other kinds of freedom are permitted. You are free to be a drunkard, an idler, a coward, a backbiter, a fornicator; but you are not free to think for yourselves. Your opinion on every subject of any conceivable importance is dictated for you by the pukka sahib's code.
>
> (p. 66)

Orwell spells out the sahib's code whereas E.M. Forster in *A Passage to India* does not. This does not seem to me inartistic explicitness, but a response to changed conditions. The code becomes more prominent and necessary to the British when it is more threatened.

Orwell conveys his criticism of imperialism with the help of his 'hero', John Flory. Flory is an exceptional European at Kyauktada in that he does not subscribe to the values of the pukka sahib held by the other Anglo-Indians. In the scene quoted above, Orwell presented Flory too ;

> Flory pushed back his chair and stood up. It must not, it could not—no, it simply should not go on any longer ! He must get out of this room quickly, before something happened inside his head and he began to smash the furniture and throw bottles at the pictures. Dull boozing witless porkers ! Was it possible that they could go on week after week, year after year, repeating word for word the same evil-minded drivel, like a parody of a fifth-rate story in *Blackwoods* ? Would none of them *ever* think of anything new to say ? Oh, what a place, what people ! What a civilization is this of ours—this godless civilization founded on whisky, *Blackwood's* and the 'Bonzo' pictures ! God have mercy on us, for all of us are part of it.
>
> (pp. 31-2)

Flory's thoughts run counter to the articulated attitudes of his fellow nationals. Orwell notes them and leaves the reader to see the contrast he implies between the values of Flory and those of the other Europeans. Flory, however, does not express his heterodox thoughts openly and, as a consequence, his attitudes are not a part of the drama, not a part of the cut and thrust of the dialogue. This reduces the force of Orwell's criticism of imperialistic values, but is inevitable, given Flory's character. Flory feels keenly the want of personal freedom in a colony and realizes that he can maintain harmonious associations with his fellow Europeans only if he conforms to their values, at least outwardly. He does not have the courage to oppose them openly or the personality to break with them. His suppression of his true self would have been an unbearable psychic burden if it were not for his conversations with Veraswami, the Indian doctor :

> 'Seditious ?' Flory said. '*I'm* not seditious. I don't want the Burmans to drive us out of this country. God forbid ! I'm here to make money, like everyone else. All I object to is the slimy white man's burden humbug. The pukka sahib pose. It's so boring. Even those bloody fools at the Club might be better company if we weren't all of us living a lie the whole time.'
>
> 'But' my dear friend, what lie are you living ?'

'Why, of course, the lie that we're here to uplift our poor black brothers instead of to rob them. I suppose it's a natural enough lie. But it corrupts us, it corrupts us in ways you can't imagine. There's an everlasting sense of being a sneak and a liar that torments us and drives us to justify ourselves night and day. It's at the bottom of half our beastliness to the natives. We Anglo-Indians could be almost bearable if we'd only admit that we're thieves and go on thieving without any humbug.'

The doctor, very pleased, nipped his thumb and forefinger together. 'The weakness of your argument, my dear friend,' he said, beaming at his own irony, 'The weakness appears to be, that you are *not* thieves.'

(pp. 37-8)

This is a moment of complete candour. Flory and Dr. Veraswami are shown to be close and trusted friends. Each man in turn, almost consciously letting the momentum of the argument sweep him along, comes out with statements which represent his true self. The frankness of both wins the sympathy of the reader. In Flory's conversations with Dr. Veraswami, Orwell dramatises directly Flory's heterodox views and his own criticism of imperialism. In a way, Flory embodies Orwell's own radical values. Through him, Orwell performs the necessary task of embodying his touchstones in character and, at the same time, presents him objectively as a distinctive individual. Malcolm Muggeridge simplifies Orwell's achievement when he says "Flory is, of course, Orwell himself."[15] Orwell and Flory are not one and the same person, though their attitudes overlap. In this argument, Orwell notes as a part of his authorial commentary, "the Englishman was bitterly anti English and the Indian fanatically loyal" (p. 38). Both characters, in Orwell's view, occupy extremist positions. Orwell is critical of all his characters, including his 'hero'. He himself would be less hard on the Anglo-Indians ; as a part of his authorial commentary, he wrote a little earlier in the book :

Living and working among Orientals would try the temper of a saint. And all of them, the officials particularly, knew

> what it was to be baited and insulted. Almost every day, when Westfield or Mr. Macgregor or even Maxwell went down the street, the High School boys, with their young yellow faces—faces smooth as gold coins, full of that meddening contempt that sits so naturally on the Mongolian face—sneered at them as they went past, sometimes hooted after them with hyena like laughter. The life of the Anglo-Indian officials is not all jam. In comfortless camp, in sweltering offices, in gloomy dakbungalows smelling of dust and earth-oil, they earn, perhaps, the right to be a little disagreeable.
>
> (p. 33)

This line of thinking is virtually Kiplingesque. George Orwell was also Eric Blair, an Englishman educated at public schools (Wellington and Eton), which "imbued him with an enthusiasm for the Raj, respect for authority, belief in discipline and action, and all that is loosely termed the public-school spirit"[16] Significantly he never wholly abandoned his original name. Yet this Kiplingesque-Blair element is not much in evidence. It is George Orwell, not Eric Blair, who is in control of the novel and he is virtually unsparing in his exposure of imperialism, though he was less severe in his later non-fictional writings.

Flory's whole character and every stage of his life is important to Orwell to convey his indictment of imperialism. Orwell seems to have been anxious to depict Flory with complete realism, to avoid making him seem a hero, more anxious than E.M. Forster in respect of Fielding in *A Passage to India*. Feilding's appearance is attractive whereas Flory's face is disfigured by a hideous birthmark. Both develop relationships with "natives" instead of keeping exclusively to their fellow nationals, but Flory lacks Fielding's courage. Orwell suggests that the imperial situation is so noxious that it maims and later ruins men like Flory. Flory is an ordinary decent man but he is driven to reticence, even hypocrisy, in relations with his fellow Europeans because the sahibs are so nasty. His only confidant is Dr. Veraswami but he is unable to be a true friend of the Indian doctor. "Every European in India is ex-officio or rather ex-colore, a good fellow" (p. 32) and Flory thinks that Veraswami is "a good fellow", that he is the equal of

Europeans. Yet he remains silent when the Anglo-Indians oppose the proposal to elect a native member to the Kyauktada Club, when they (especially Ellis) denigrate the Indian, who is the only suitable candidate. He even signs a Club notice insulting his friend and can do no more than apologise for it in private. Flory's pusillanimity is particularly reprehensible in this matter because he knows that Veraswami needs the prestige of being able to associate with Europeans to combat the machinations of his enemy U Po Kyin, the Burmese Sub-divisional magistrate. Flory himself is aware that he has no "guts" and this is among the failings which generate in him a self-contempt :

> 'Cur, spineless cur,' Flory was thinking to himself; without heat, however, for he was too accustomed to the thought. 'Sneaking, idling, boozing, fornicating, soul-examining, self-pitying cur. All those fools at the Club, those dull louts to whom you are so pleased to think yourself superior—they are all better than you, every man of them. At least they are men in their oafish way. Not cowards, not liars. Not half-dead and rotting. But you . . .' (p. 59)

These thoughts are part of the memorable scene in which a "pariah cur" takes "a dislike to Flory's house and had settled down to bay at it systematically" (p. 59). Orwell symbolically suggests that Flory's role in human society is equivalent to the cur's position as a pariah.

The imperial, situation drives Flory to drink and womanizing. He has a Burmese mistress, Ma Hla May, and, in depicting their relationship, Orwell takes the reader into the bedroom :

> 'You only like me because I am a white man and have money,' he said.
>
> 'Master, I love you, I love you more than anything in the world. Why do you say that ? Have I not always been faithful to you ?'
>
> 'You have a Burmese lover.'
>
> 'Ugh !' Ma Hla May affected to shudder at the thought.

> 'To think of their horrible brown hands, touching me! I should die if a Burman touched me!'
>
> 'Liar.'
>
> He put his hand on her breast. Privately, Ma Hla May did not like this, for it reminded her that her breasts existed—the ideal of a Burmese woman being to have no breasts. She lay and let him do as he wished with her, quite passive yet pleased and faintly smiling, like a cat which allows one to stroke it. Flory's embraces meant nothing to her (Ba Pe, Ko S'la's younger brother, was secretly her lover), yet she was bitterly hurt when he neglected them. Sometimes she had even put love-philtres in his food. It was the idle concubine's life that she loved, and the visits to her village dressed in all her finery, when she could boast of her position as a 'bo-kadaw'—a white man's wife; for she had persuaded everyone, herself included, that she was Flory's legal wife.
>
> When Flory had done with her he turned away, jaded and ashamed, and lay silent with his left hand covering his birthmark. (pp. 51-2)

Orwell boldly deals with an intimate inter-racial relationship between sexes, an aspect of life in a colony which Forster skirts in *A Passage to India* and which Kipling handles less candidly. Orwell reveals a remarkable insight into the mind and heart of both the Englishman and the Burmese. They are both aware of hypocrisies in their association but continue to meet sexually. Both know that their liaison is disgraceful but nevertheless continue it. Particularly impressive are Orwell's perceptions into the complex being of the woman from a race and culture alien to him, into her aesthetic sense, her divided allegiances, her dissimulation and primitive thinking. Ma Hla May too is corrupted by the imperial system : Flory's position as a member of the ruling race, a potent attraction for her, and his character contribute to undermine her moral values. But I wouldn't, and Orwell doesn't, ascribe her degeneracy wholly to the imperial system : prostitution is proverbially the oldest profession and was practised by Easterners before Westerners had anything to do with them ; it is a human failing.

The imperial situation imposes a terrible loneliness on Flory and, at the same time, he cannot bring himself to leave it :

> He had no tie with Europe now, except the tie of books. For he had realised that merely to go back to England was no remedy for loneliness ; he had grasped the special nature of the hell that is reserved for Anglo-Indians. Ah, those poor prosing old wrecks in Bath and Cheltenham ! Those tomb-like boarding houses with Anglo-Indians littered about in all stages of decomposition, all talking and talking about what happened in Boggleyalah in '88 ! Poor devils, they know what it means to have left one's heart in an alien and hated country. There was, he saw clearly, only one way out. To find someone who would share his life in Burma—but really share his inner, secret life, carry away the same memories as he carried from Burma. Someone who would love Burma as he loved it and hate it as he hated it. Who would help him to live with nothing hidden, nothing unexpressed. Someone who understood him : a friend, that was what it came down to. (p. 69)

Flory had no 'friend who understood him'. The sahibs were a class apart. Ko S'la was a devoted Burmese servant, but no friend. Ma Hla May was merely an object to satisfy Flory's sexual desires. Dr. Veraswami was his only friend, but not really a companion. Their friendship was based, not on intellectual understanding, but on sympathy and tolerance. Thus, when Elizabeth, the niece of the Lackersteens, arrives in Kyauktada, Flory sees the possibility of winning a wife who will be both friend and companion. He sees her as offering an escape from his lonely, secretive and degenerate way of life and an opportunity for regeneration. He dismisses Ma Hla May and prepares to court Elizabeth. Unfortunately, Elizabeth's character was such that she could not be Flory's salvation. She had spent two terms at "a very expensive boarding-school" (p. 86) and this experience had permanently fixed her character as a superficial snob. Flory himself has an understanding respect for Orientals and Oriental civilizations and naturally thinks that his future wife will share his interests. He takes Elizabeth to see *pwe*, a Burmese dance drama, to the Bazaar and Li Yeik's shop. But she is indifferent and insults the Burmese. Flory, however, is not discouraged :

> Yet with Elizabeth serious talk seemed impossible. It was as though there had been a spell upon them that made all their conversation lapse into banality ; gramophone records, dogs, tennis racquets—all that desolating Club-chatter. She seemed not to *want* to talk of anything but that. He had only to touch upon a subject of any conceivable interest to hear the evasion, the 'Is shan't play', coming into her voice. Her taste in books appalled him when he discovered it. Yet she was young, he reminded himself, and had she not drunk white wine and talked of Marcel Proust under the Paris plane trees? Later, no doubt, she would understand him and give him the companionship he needed. Perhaps it was only that he had not won her confidence yet.
>
> (pp. 111-12)

He romanticises her stay in Paris and makes excuses for her. Love makes him blind to her true character.

The association of Flory and Elizabeth grows warm only on three occasions, and these occur when Flory appears a hero in her conventional eyes. The first is when he meets her for the first time and she thinks that he has performed an extraordinarily brave deed in saving her from a buffalo, a fearsome-looking but really harmless animal. The second is during the shooting expedition. Orwell's writing becomes unusually powerful and suggestive :

> Flory took one of the little green corpses to show to Elizabeth. 'Look at it, Aren't they lovely things ? The most beautiful bird in Asia.'
>
> Elizabeth touched its smooth feathers with her finger-tip. It filled her with better envy, because she had not shot it. And yet it was curious, but she felt almost an adoration for Flory now that she had seen how he could shoot.
>
> 'Just look at its breast-feathers ; like a jewel. It's murder to shoot them. The Burmese say that when you kill one of these birds they vomit, meaning to say, "Look, here is all I

possess, and I've taken nothing of yours. Why do you kill me ?" I've never seen one do it, I must admit.'

'Are they good to eat ?'

'Very. Even so, I always feel it's a shame to kill them.'

'I wish I could do it like you do !' she said enviously.

'It's only a knack, you'll soon pick it up. You know how to hold your gun, and that's more than most people do when they start.'

(pp. 156-57)

Orwell captures a whole complex of feelings—the ardour of Flory and Elizabeth for each other, their enthusiasm for hunting and Flory's regret for killing beautiful pigeons. Orwell suggests Elizabeth's cold-bloodedness ; it strikes the reader but not Flory. Her callousness and Flory's unawareness are both portents. The third occasion when the association of Flory and Elizabeth grows warm, occurs towards the end of the novel. Ellis hurts a Burmese boy and a Burmese mob attacks the Club. Flory escapes from the besieged Club, swims across the river, directs the operations of the Police against the mob, and the mob finally disperses. He thus saves the Europeans and becomes a hero in their eyes. Elizabeth's feelings for him, however, do not last long. She quickly transfers her interest to the playboy Verrall when he arrives to take charge temporarily of the Military Police at Kyauktada. The reader finds the quick change of heart convincing. Elizabeth's feelings for Flory had never been deep and she was disturbed that Flory was not quite a sahib. In her view, Flory was a "highbrow" and it was a bond between Verrall and her that he "detested anything 'highbrow' even more than she did. He told her once that he had not read a book since he was eighteen and that indeed he 'loathed' books" (p. 203) Moreover, the hunting expedition has already suggested to the reader that Elizabeth is capable of taking cold-blooded opportunistic decisions. The association of Verrall and Elizabeth, however, ends soon as Verrall's intentions, true to his type, were not serious or honourable. After Verrall leaves Kyauktada, Elizabeth returns to Flory and he is so much in love and so humble that he accepts her. But she is soon completely alienated when Ma Hla May, at the instigations of U Po Kyin, shames Flory in church. It is ironical that the woman Flory sees as his source of salvation, should have a character cut out to be the burra memsahib she finally becomes as Mr. Macgregor's wife. Flory feels that he cannot continue to live in the unsatisfactory way he did earlier and commits suicide. The process of thinking whereby a seasoned man like Flory decides to take away his own life, is rendered a trifle perfunctorily and the suicide itself appears a trifle melodramatic, but only a trifle. It is not inconceivable that a man life Flory, sensitive and decent, though seasoned, could reach the end of his tether in the given circumstances. The imperial situation finally kills the only decent European in Kyauktada. Orwell suggests that decency has no place in an imperial situation, that there is no hope for a decent man in an imperial situation ; once he enters it, he is doomed.

Flory's fate enacts the tragedy of the want of personal freedom in a colony and there is nothing in colonial literature to equal Orwell's rendering of this theme. In *A Passage to India,* Forster handled the same theme and he came to much the same conclusion : Mrs. Moore and Adela Quested, honest and liberal, try to be different from the Anglo-Indians, but their plans fail, they cannot find a niche in India and have to leave ; Fielding has a character like theirs but he is able to remain only after surrendering to Anglo-India at the end. But in *A Passage to India,* this theme is secondary and not central as in *Burmese Days.* Orwell also valuably conveys the economic exploitation, the basic motive of imperialism, which is virtually absent in *A Passage to India* and in Kipling's fiction. Orwell himself said of Kipling in his celebrated essay : ". . . he had never had any grasp of the economic forces underlying imperial expansion. It is notable that Kipling does not seem to realize, any more than the average soldier or colonial administrator, that an empire is primarily a money-making concern."[17] Orwell criticised F. Tennyson Jesse's book, *The Story of Burma,* in these terms : "No one would infer from your book that the British had done anything worse than be a little stupid and sometimes follow mistaken policies. Nothing about the economic milching of the country via such concerns as the Burma Oil Company, nor about the disgusting social behaviour of the British till very recently."[18] Orwell makes good the deficiencies he finds in Kipling and F. Tennyson Jesse. It is significant that Flory is a timber merchant, Lackersteen the local manager of a timber firm, Ellis the local manager of yet another company, Maxwell the acting Divisional Forest officer. Timber is to Burma in *Burmese Days* what ivory was to the Congo in Conrad's *Heart of Darkness* and silver was to Costaguana in Conrad's *Nostromo.* It is the actual raw wealth which private individuals, colonial companies and imperial powers covet, as well as a symbolic centre for their self-aggrandising motives. The fundamental importance of commercial activity, of "money-making", among the Europeans in Burma is put explicitly by Flory in his words to Dr. Veraswami which I quoted earlier : I'm here to make money like everyone else", "the lie that we're here to uplift our poor black brothers instead of to rob them" and so on.

Orwell opens up more aspects of imperialism through his "native" characters. U Po Kyin is the most important character among the Burmese. He is a convincingly Burmese villain. He advances himself by ruthless intrigue and, at the same time, he wants to ensure that "he would return to the earth in male human shape—for a woman ranks at about the same level as a rat or a frog—or at best as some dignified beast such as an elephant" (p. 7) by means of meritorious deeds. He is bold in that, in a colonial environment, his misdeeds extend to the master race. His insight into the psychology of the sahibs in cynical and penetrating :

> 'Nonsense, nonsense,' said U Po Kyin comfortably. No European cares anything about proofs. When a man has a black face, suspicion is proof. A few anonymous letters will work wonders. It is only a question of persisting ; accuse, go on accusing—that is the way with Europeans. . . .'
>
> (p. 11)

His insight is proved to be true when he uses it to discredit Dr. Veraswami in the eyes of the Europeans and succeeds. Even though he is a European, when Flory stands in U Po Kyin's way, the Burmese decides to nullify Flory's influence from which Veraswami benefits ; he uses Ma Hla May to disgrace Flory in front of all the Europeans. He rises professionally and socially ; he does not 'control his rulers' as Jeffrey Meyers asserts,[19] but deceives them. He is promoted from Government Clerk to Sub-divisional Magistrate and, then, to Deputy Assistant Commissioner. He is elected a member of the prestigious Club of the Europeans and is finally, decorated by the Government at a durbar in Rangoon. His success is a mordant criticism of the superficiality of British colonial administration and British colonial society.

Dr. Veraswami is the most respect-worthy character in the novel, taking into account both the Europeans and the "natives", and this is a measure of Orwell's broad-mindedness. Veraswami is more decent than Flory and more balanced He takes liquor in moderate quantities, and leads an honourable professional and domestic life. He is magnanimous : he forgives Flory's insincerity and cowardice at the Club. But the imperial situation spoils his character too and maims it. His colonial English education makes him a pro-British fanatic and a denigrator of his own people. At the same time, neither is he admitted into colonial British society because he is a "native", nor does he share in Burmese society. Thus, he belongs nowhere. He is vulnerable, an easy target for U Po Kyin, if Flory were not his friend. At the end of the book, Flory ennobled by his love for Elizabeth and encouraged by the esteem of his fellow Europeans after he saved them from the Burmese mob, proposes Dr. Veraswami's election as a member of the Club, but the moment is too late for this to be of any use to Flory or Veraswami. Before the election takes place, Flory falls and, with Flory, Veraswami falls. U Po Kyin turns European opinion against Veraswami, the doctor is reverted to the rank of Assistant Surgeon and transferred to Mandalay where he leads an ignoble life. It is U Po Kyin who is elected the native member of the Kyauktada Club.

Veraswami's characterisation verges on comic caricature and comes close to a portrait of a Babu. Not only are his imperialistic opinions shown up as absurd, he has peculiar mannerisms and speaks a "queer English" (p. 47) ; here he warns Flory about U Po Kyin :

> 'Nevertheless, beware of his calumnies, my friend. Do not underrate him. He will know how to strike at you. He is a crocodile. And like the crocodile'—the doctor nipped his thumb and finger impressively ; his images became mixed sometimes—'like the crocodile, he strikes always at the weakest spot !'
>
> (pp. 46-7)

The caricature-like quality is amusing, but the reader never loses his respect for Dr. Veraswami because of his worthiness. Moreover, Veraswami proves to be an accurate judge of U Po Kyin's character, whereas the normal Europeans are fooled. Even Flory is half-blind to U Po Kyin's true nature because of racial arrogance and pays for it. Though Veraswami's character redeems the pessimism of the novel, the overall and final impression is black ; Veraswami, like Flory, is ruined in the end ; the colonial situation does not permit the worthy to prosper, whatever the race and political status.

In describing Asians, Orwell often resorts to animal imagery.[20] Ma Kin, U Po Kyin's wife, has a "simian face" (p. 13). The Indian butler at the Club has "liquid, yellow-irised eyes like those of a dog" (p. 20). Referring to Veraswami, Orwell says : "The tears had actually started into his eyes, and these, magnified by his spectacles, beamed upon Flory like the liquid eyes of a dog" (p. 142-3). This kind of imagery reveals a want of sympathy for the Asians and even a streak of conventional racial prejudice. As Frantz Fanon observes, "when the settler seeks to describe the native fully in exact terms he constantly refers to the bestiary."[21] It is only rarely that Orwell uses animal imagery to describe Europeans and then it is not offensive in the same degree. He says of Maxwell : "With heavy limbs and thick white eyelashes he reminded one of a cart-house colt" (p. 21).

Orwell's use of animal imagery is one manifestation of a certain harshness in his portrayal of the imperial situation, particularly with regard to the Burmese and their country. Veraswami is an Indian. The Burmese prominent in the novel are a villain, U Po Kyin, and a prostitute, Ma Hla May ; Ma Kin is a pious but weak character, and also unimportant. One could suggest the dimension missed by Orwell by referring to the historian G.E. Harvey and Rudyard Kipling. In *British Rule in Burma* Harvey wrote : "there is, in Burmese life, not only a beauty that delights the eye but also a dignity which makes one proud of the human race."[22] The British soldier in Kipling's Mandalay' says :

> I've a neater, sweeter maiden in a cleaner, greener land !
>
> On the road to Mandalay......[23]

'Mandalay' was, in fact, Orwell's "favourite poem,"[24] but it has not appreciably influenced him in writing *Burmese Days.*

Both the power and harshness of the novel derive from Orwell's extreme disillusionment with imperialism and the reformer's intention to drive home its evils. In *The Road to Wigan Pier*, he wrote :

> I was in the Indian Police five years, and by the end of that time I hated the imperialism I was serving with a bitterness which a probably cannot make clear . . . it is not possible to be part of such a system without recognizing it as unjustifiable tyranny......For five years I had been part of an oppressive system, and it had left me with a bad conscience. . . . I was conscious of an immense weight of guilt that I had got to expiate.[25]

Orwell's bitter hatred and guilt account for the ultimately chilling impact of *Burmese Days* but these feelings have also produced a distinguished first novel. It does not achieve greatness of *A Passage to India* or Kipling's *Kim*, but it is more valuable than any of Conrad's Malayan novels. It is on a par with Joyce Cary's African novels or E.M. Forster's pre-War novels.

NOTES

1. Quoted from Ian Hamilton, 'Making Up His Mind' : *New Statesman*, 24 September 1976, p. 414.
2. Ian Hamilton, op. cit., p. 414.
3. It was published in Penguin Books (not for the first time) in 1967 and reprinted in 1969, 1972, 1973, 1975 (twice).

4. E.g., Joffrey Meyers, 'The Ethics of Responsibility : Orwell's *Burmese Days*' ; *University Review*, Vol. XXV, December 1968, p. 84 ; Meyers agrees with Orwell's view quoted in note 5. Raymond Williams ignores *Burmese Days* in his *George Orwell* (London : Fontana, 1971). Malcolm Muggeridge's judgement that *Burmese Days* is "the most satisfactory of Orwell's novels" is exceptional. See Malcolm Muggeridge, 'Introduction' : George Orwell, *Burmese Days* (New York : Time Incorporated, 1962 ed.), p. xv.

5. "When I was about sixteen......I wanted to write enormous naturalistic novels with unhappy endings, full of detailed descriptions and arresting similes, and also full of purple passages in which words were used partly for the sake of sound. And in fact my first completed novel, *Burmese Days*, which I wrote when I was thirty but projected much earlier, is rather that kind of book " George Orwell, 'Why I Write' (1947) : *Collected Essays* (London : Secker and Warburg, 1961 ed), p. 447.

6. Bernard Crick, 'The Road to 1984' : *Times Literary Supplement*, 3 June 1977, p. 686.

7. Orwell, 'Why I Write' : *Collected Essays*, p. 440.

8. George Orwell, *The Road to Wigan Pier* (New York: Berkley Publishing Corporation, 1961 ed.), p. 126; Orwell, 'Shooting an Elephant' (1936) : *Collected Essays*, p. 15.

9. Orwell, letter to F. Tennyson Jesse, 14 March 1946 : Sonia Orwell and Ian Angus (ed.), *The Collected Essays, Journalism and Letters of George Orwell* (London : Penguin, 1980 ed.), Vol. IV, p. 142.

10. Orwell, *The Road to Wigan Pier*, p. 128.

11. Orwell, 'Shooting an Elephant' : *Collected Essays*, p. 15.

12. George Orwell, *Burmese Days* (London: Penguin, 1967 ed.), pp. 29-31 ; all later quotations from the novel are from this edition and their page-numbers are noted in my text.

13. Leonard Woolf, *Growing : An Autobiography of the years 1904 1911* London : Hogarth Press, 1964 ed.), p. 510.
14. E.M. Forster, *A Passage to India* (London : Penguin, 1959 ed.), p. 24 ; my italics.
15. Malcolm Muggeridge, 'Introduction' : Orwell, *Burmese Days*, p. xii. Cf. "There can be no doubt he [Flory] is meant to be Orwell himself". Editor's Preface, ibid., p. viii. Edward M. Thomas virtually subscribes to this view : "... Flory, the hero, like Orwell's later heroes, is Orwell without his quality of moral courage—perhaps one could say without his dimension of writer, since this was the role in which he most often chose to oppose injustice". See Edward M. Thomas, *Orwell* (Edinburgh & London : Oliver & Boyd, 1965), p. 9.
16. Shamsul Islam, *Chronicles of the Raj* (London : Macmillan, 1979), p 63.
17. George Orwell, 'Rudyard Kipling' : Sonia Orwell and Ian Angus (ed.), *The Collected Essays, Journalism and Letters of George Orwell*, Vol. II, p. 217.
18. Orwell, letter to F. Tennyson Jesse, 14 March 1946 : ibid , Vol. IV, p. 142.
19. Jeffrey Meyers, op. cit.. p. 85.
20. Cf. George Woodcock, *The Crystal Spirit : A Study of George Orwell* (London : Penguin, 1970 ed.), p. 82. When I read George Woodcock's fine pages on *Burmese Days* after writing my essay, I found that he too had noted Orwell's use of animal imagery, but he does not draw the conclusions which I do.
21. Frantz Fanon, *The Wretched of the Earth* (London: Penguin, 1967), p. 33.
22. Quoted from *The New Encyclopaedia Britannica* (Helen Hemingway Benton, 15th ed., 1974), p. 189.
23. T.S. Eliot (ed.), *A Choice of Kipling's Verse* (London : Faber and Faber, 1963 ed.), p. 189.
24. Malcolm Muggeridge, 'Introduction' : op. cit., p. xi.
25. Orwell, *The Road to Wigan Pier*, pp. 124-5, 127-8.